The Bases of Design

Walter Crane

Alpha Editions

This edition published in 2024

ISBN : 9789366384511

Design and Setting By
Alpha Editions
www.alphaedis.com
Email - info@alphaedis.com

As per information held with us this book is in Public Domain.
This book is a reproduction of an important historical work. Alpha Editions uses the best technology to reproduce historical work in the same manner it was first published to preserve its original nature. Any marks or number seen are left intentionally to preserve its true form.

Contents

PREFACE ....- 1 -

AUTHOR'S NOTE ON THE PRESENT
EDITION ....- 3 -

CHAPTER I.—OF THE
ARCHITECTURAL BASIS ....- 4 -

CHAPTER II.—OF THE UTILITY
BASIS AND INFLUENCE ....- 38 -

CHAPTER III.—OF THE INFLUENCE
OF MATERIAL AND METHOD ....- 71 -

CHAPTER IV.—ON THE INFLUENCE
OF CONDITIONS IN DESIGN ....- 94 -

CHAPTER V.—OF THE CLIMATIC
INFLUENCE IN DESIGN—CHIEFLY
IN REGARD TO COLOUR AND
PATTERN ....- 120 -

CHAPTER VI.—OF THE RACIAL
INFLUENCE IN DESIGN ....- 140 -

CHAPTER VII.—OF THE SYMBOLIC
INFLUENCE, OR EMBLEMATIC
ELEMENT IN DESIGN ....- 162 -

CHAPTER VIII.—OF THE GRAPHIC INFLUENCE, OR NATURALISM IN DESIGN .... - 186 -

CHAPTER IX.—OF THE INDIVIDUAL INFLUENCE IN DESIGN .... - 212 -

CHAPTER X.—OF THE COLLECTIVE INFLUENCE .... - 240 -

PREFACE

THE substance of the following chapters originally formed a series of lectures addressed to the students of the Manchester Municipal School of Art during my tenure of the directorship of Design at that institution.

The field covered is an extensive one, and I am conscious that many branches of my subject are only touched, whilst others are treated in a very elementary manner. Every chapter, indeed, might be expanded into a volume, under such far-reaching headings, to give to each section anything like adequate treatment.

My main object, however, has been to trace the vital veins and nerves of relationship in the arts of design, which, like the sap from the central stem, springing from connected and collective roots, out of a common ground, sustain and unite in one organic whole the living tree.

In an age when, owing to the action of certain economic causes—the chiefest being commercial competition—the tendency is to specialize each branch of design, which thus becomes isolated from the rest, I feel it is most important to keep in mind the real fundamental connection and essential unity of art: and though we may, as students and artists, in practice be intent upon gathering the fruit from the particular branch we desire to make our own, we should never be insensible to its relation to other branches, its dependence upon the main stem and the source of its life at the root.

Otherwise we are, I think, in danger of becoming mechanical in our work, or too narrowly technical, while, as a collective result of such narrowness of view, the art of the age, to which each individual contributes, shows a want of both imaginative harmony and technical relation with itself, when unity of effect and purpose is particularly essential, as in the design and decoration of both public and private buildings, not to speak of the larger significance of art as the most permanent record of the life and ideals of a people.

My illustrations are drawn from many sources, and consist of a large proportion of those originally used for the lectures, only that instead of the rough charcoal sketches done at the time, careful pen drawings have been made of many of the subjects in addition to the photographs and other authorities.

It may be noted that I have freely used both line and tone blocks in the text and throughout the book, although I advocate the use of line drawings only with type in books wherein completeness of organic ornamental character is the object. Such a book as this, however, being rather in the nature of a tool or auxiliary to a designer's workshop, can hardly be regarded from that point of view. The scheme of the work, which necessitates the gathering together of so many and varied illustrations as diverse in scale, subject, and treatment as the historic periods which they represent, would itself preclude a consistent decorative treatment, and it has been found necessary to reproduce many of the illustrations from their original form in large scale drawings on brown paper touched with white, as well as from photographs which necessarily print as tone-blocks.

I have to thank Mr. Gleeson White for his valuable help in many ways, as well as in obtaining permission from various owners of copyright to use photographs and other illustrations, and also the publishers, who have allowed me the use of blocks in some instances—Mr. George Allen for a page from "The Faerie Queene"; Messrs. Bradbury, Agnew and Co. for the use of the "Punch" drawings; and Messrs. J. S. Virtue and Co. for the use of photographs of carpet weaving and glass blowing, which were specially taken for "The Art Journal." My thanks are also due to Mr. Metford Warner (Messrs. Jeffrey and Co.) for the use of his photo-lithographs of my wallpaper designs issued by his firm; to Mr. R. Phené Spiers for the use of his sketch of the iron balustrade from Rothenburg; to Mr. T. J. Cobden-Sanderson for photographs of two of his recent bookbindings; to the executors of the late Rev. W. H. Creeny for permission to reproduce two of the illustrations from his "Monumental Brasses on the Continent of Europe" (now published by Mr. B. T. Batsford); also to Mr. Harold Rathbone, who kindly allows me to reproduce the cartoons by Ford Madox Brown in his possession; to Mr. J. Sylvester Sparrow for the practical notes on painting glass; and to Mr. Emery Walker for help in several ways in the preparation of the book.

WALTER CRANE.

KENSINGTON,
November, 1897.

AUTHOR'S NOTE ON THE PRESENT EDITION

THIS reprint of "The Bases of Design" gives me an opportunity to correct a few errors which had inadvertently crept in on its first appearance, and also to add a word here and there.

I venture to hope that the book may prove more useful and accessible to students in its present form.

WALTER CRANE.

KENSINGTON,
November, 1901.

CHAPTER I.—OF THE ARCHITECTURAL BASIS

WHEN we approach the study of Design, from whatever point of view, and whatsoever our ultimate aim and purpose, we can hardly fail to be impressed with the vast variety and endless complexity of the forms which the term (Design) covers, understanding it in its widest and fullest sense.

From the simplest linear pattern, or bone scratchings of primitive man, to the most splendid achievements in mural decoration of the Italian Renascence—or, shall we say, from the grass mat of the first plaiter to the finest Persian carpet: or from Stonehenge to Salisbury Cathedral—the range is enormous, and were we to attempt to trace, step by step, the true relation between the diverse and multitudinous characteristics which such contrasts suggest, we should be tracing the course of the development of human thought and history themselves.

When we stand amazed in this labyrinth—this enchanted and beautiful wood of human invention which the history of art displays, we might be content to gaze at the loveliness of particular forms there, and simply enjoy, like children, the beauty of the trees and flowers; gathering here and there at random, and casting them aside again when we were tired, without a thought as to their true significance.

If, however, we desire to find some clue to the labyrinth—something which will explain it in part, at least, something which will give us a key to the relation of these manifold forms, and enable us to place them in harmonious order and coherence, we shall presently ask:

(1) How and whence they derived their leading characteristics?

(2) Upon what basis have they been built up? and

(3) What have been the chief influences which have determined, and still determine, their varieties?

Let us try to address ourselves to these questions, since, I believe, even if we only end as we begin, by inquiry, that, in the course of that inquiry, by study, by comparison, and careful observation, we shall be able greatly to clear our path, and find much to help us as individual students and practical workers in art.

(1) The first arts are, of course, those of pure utility, which spring from the primal physical necessities of man: which are concerned in the maintenance of life itself—the art or craft of the hunter and the fisherman, the tiller of the soil, the hewer of wood and the drawer of water: but seeing that next to

securing sufficiency of food, the efforts of man are directed towards providing himself with shelter, both of roof and raiment, and since most of the arts of the creative sort must be practised under shelter of some kind, and that all of them contribute in some way towards the building or adornment of such shelter, I think we shall find the true basis and controlling influences, which have been paramount in the development of decorative design, *in the form and character of the dwellings of man* and their accessories; from the temples he has raised to enshrine his highest ideals—these temples themselves being but larger and more monumental dwellings—to the tomb, his last dwelling-place. We shall find, in short, the original and controlling bases of design in architecture, the queen and mother of all the arts.

In asserting this one does not lose sight of the view that *all art is, primarily, the projection or precipitation in material form of man's emotional and intellectual nature*; but, being projected and taking definite shape, it becomes subject to certain controlling forces of nature, of material, of condition, which re-act upon the mind; and it is with these controlling forces and conditions, and the distinctions which arise out of them, that we are now concerned.

Such distinctions as exist, for instance, in the feeling, the plan and construction of those patterns intended to be laid upon the floors (as in carpets or tiles), and such as are intended to cover ceilings and walls (as in plaster-work, textile hangings or wall papers), obviously arise from the relative positions of floor, walls, and ceilings, and the differences between horizontal and vertical positions; and these conditions are necessarily part and parcel of the constructional conditions of the dwelling itself.

The first shelter may be said to have been the shelter of nature without art—the TREE and the CAVE, the first homes of man; although he was probably not by any means the first animal to hide among the woods and the rocks, since he had many and formidable foes to dispute with or disturb him in possession. It is noticeable that such art as is associated with this strange and remote chapter of man's existence on the earth—the art-instinct which impelled the primitive hunter to incise the bone and stone implements he used with the images of the animals he hunted—is purely graphic, and does not show any feeling of that adaptive ornamental quality characteristic of what we call decorative design, which would seem to belong to a more highly organized condition of society. "Among the primitive Greeks," remarks Messrs. Guhl and Köner in their Life of the Greeks and Romans, "fountains and trees, caves and mountains, were considered as seats of the gods, and revered accordingly, even without being changed into divine habitations by the art of man." But, as proving literally that art springs out of nature, the cave itself led to a development of architecture, as in some early Greek tombs where the cave, or cleft in the rocks, is utilized and added to by masonry; or where the rock itself was carved and hollowed, as in the rock-cut temples of Egypt and India. To which some trace the origin of columnar architecture.

The TENT of the Asiatic wandering tribes, and the wattled and wooden HUT of the western and northern, come next in the order of human dwellings, and not only may we trace certain types of pattern design to both sources, but it would seem as if both the tent and the hut, and perhaps the wagon of the Aryans, had had their influence upon the more substantial stone structures which succeeded them. When tribes became communities, townships were founded, and more fixed and settled habits of life prevailed.

DIAGRAM TO SHOW THE THREE TYPICAL FORMS OF ARCHITECTURE:

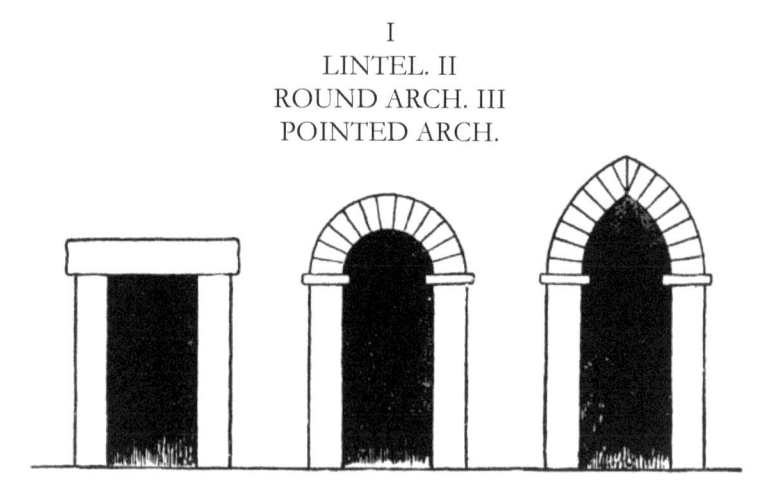

I
LINTEL. II
ROUND ARCH. III
POINTED ARCH.

Now we may broadly group the principal types of architectural form and construction in three principal divisions, following Professor Ruskin, namely:

1. The architecture of the Lintel (or column and pediment).

2. The architecture of the Round Arch (or vault and dome).

3. The architecture of the Pointed Arch[1] (or vault, gable, and buttress).

Of the first we may find the simplest type in Stonehenge; we may find it in equally massive, and almost as primitive form at Mycenæ, in the famous Gate of the Lions, remarkable as being the earliest known example of Greek sculpture: we may find it more developed in the Greek temples of ancient Egypt, at Karnac, Thebes and Philæ, and we may see it in its purest form in the Parthenon at Athens.

GATE OF MYCENÆ.

The derivation and development of the Greek Doric temple from its prototype of wooden construction has frequently been demonstrated, and the tombs in Lycia furnish striking illustrations of this close imitation and perpetuation in stone of a system and details belonging to wood; and it is instructive to compare its features with corresponding parts in the Parthenon, and to observe how closely they agree. It is a curious instance of that love for and clinging to ancient and traditional forms, that with the art and all the resources of Athenian civilization, the form and construction of its temples remained much the same, and may be considered as only glorified enlargements in marble of their wooden predecessors, retaining all the characteristic details of those primitive structures.

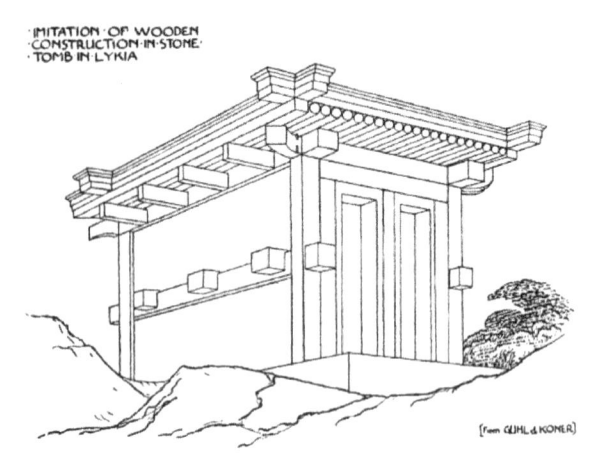

**IMITATION OF WOODEN CONSTRUCTION IN STONE
TOMB IN LYKIA,
[From GUHL & KONER].**

By these means, however, qualities of grandeur, joined with extreme simplicity, subtle proportions, and sparing, severe, but delicately chiselled ornament were gained; which, when heightened with colour in the broad and strong sunshine of Greece, seemed all sufficient, especially so when they formed the framework, or setting, of the most beautiful and noble sculpture the world has ever seen, as in the Parthenon.

To this sculpture, indeed, all the lines and proportions of the building seem to lead the eye, while it remains, whether in pediment, metope, or frieze, an essential part of the architectural effect, and is strictly slab sculpture, or what may be considered as architectural ornament, for, as I have elsewhere said, we may fairly consider figure-sculpture to have been the ornament of the Greeks: just as one might say that picture writing and hieroglyphic were the mural decorations of the Egyptians.

ORNAMENTAL LINES IN THE FRIEZE OF THE PARTHENON.

WAVE MOVEMENT & SPIRAL CURVES IN THE FRIEZE.

These sculptures were evidently designed under the influence of the strongest architectural and decorative feeling, and were constructed upon a basis of ornamental lines. There is a certain rhythm and recurrence of mass, and line, and form in them throughout, and they have all been carefully considered in relation to the places they occupy.

·METOPE· OF ·THE· PARTHENON·

·SHOWING· RELATION·&· PROPORTIONS· OF· THE·
·MASSES· IN· RELIEF· TO ·THE· GROUND·

METOPE OF THE PARTHENON, SHOWING RELATION & PROPORTIONS OF THE MASSES IN RELIEF TO THE GROUND.

It is to be noted, too, that the sculptures are placed in the *interstices of the construction*; that is to say, not on the actual bearing parts. On this point it is interesting to compare with the earlier forms of pure stone construction at Mycenæ. The lions over the Mycenæ Gate are carved upon a slab of stone placed in the triangular hollow left above the lintel to prevent it breaking under the great pressure of the heavy stones used. The triangular hollow may be seen *without* the slab in the doorway of Clytemnestra's house at Mycenæ. Here we have an early instance of the interstice left by the necessities of the construction being utilized as a decorative feature, significant in its design, showing the protecting image of the Castle of Mycenæ, much in the same way as we see the family arms sculptured over the gateways of our English mediæval castles.

Returning to the Parthenon, we see that the same principle is observable in the pediment and metope sculptures, the frieze of the cella being really a mural decoration consisting of facing slabs of marble. The building would doubtless stand without any of them, as a timber-framed house would stand without its boarding, or filling of brick or plaster; but it would be like a skeleton, or a head without its eyes—much, indeed, as time, bombardment, ravage, and the British Museum have left it now.

Before we leave the Parthenon, let me call attention to one prevailing principle, characteristic of its design in every part; for though following throughout the principles or traditions of wooden construction, no doubt its proportions and lines were consciously and carefully considered by the architect with a view to æsthetic effect. It is *the principle of recurring or re-echoing lines*, a leading principle, indeed, throughout the whole province of Design, and one on the importance and value of which it is impossible to lay too much stress.

**THE PARTHENON
[After MENGE].**

PARTHENON EASTERN PEDIMENT—SKETCH TO SHOW RELATION OF LINES OF SCULPTURE TO ANGLE OF PEDIMENT.

PARTHENON EASTERN PEDIMENT—SKETCH TO SHOW RELATION OF LINES OF SCULPTURE TO ANGLE OF PEDIMENT.

To begin with the pediment. The main outline is delicately emphasized by the mouldings of the edge, which also serve as a dripstone—the practical origin, probably, of all mouldings. The groups of sculptured figures within the recess (which further serve to express the pitch of the roof) re-echo, informally, in the lines controlling their composition, as well as in the lines of limbs and draperies, variations of the angle of the pediment. Thus, the groups of figures, full of action and variety as they are, are united and harmonized with the whole building; while, to avoid undue appearance of heaviness on the crest of the pediment and on the angles were placed anthemion bronze ornaments.

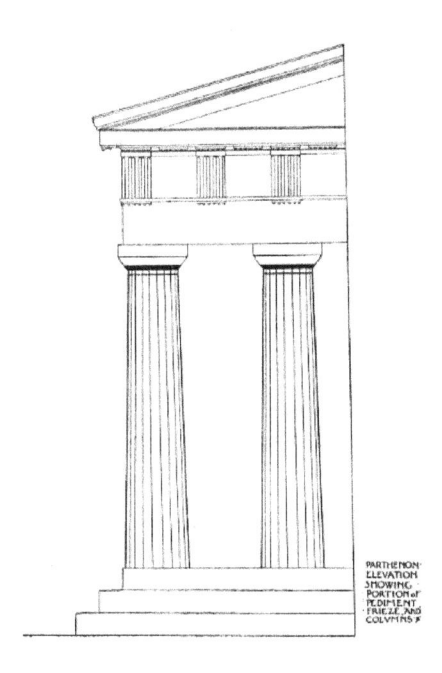

PARTHENON ELEVATION SHOWING PORTION OF PEDIMENT FRIEZE AND COLUMNS.

The cornice, again, is emphasized by mouldings marking the important horizontal lines of the building, re-echoed by the lines of the frieze, and counteracted and braced by the emphatic vertical lines of the triglyphs, and enriched by the little dentils below.

Then we come to the cap of the Doric column. It is simplicity itself. A thin square block of marble forms the abacus. The capital is a flattened circular cushion of marble, rounded at the sides in a diminishing curve to the head of the column, which terminates in a horizontal reeding. The column itself is delicately channelled with a series of lines which follow its outline, and give vertical expression to the idea of the support of the horizontal mass above, the column gradually diminishing from base to cap, entasized or slightly swelled in the middle to avoid the visual effect of running out of the perpendicular. The Doric columns spring boldly from the steps without base mouldings, the steps repeating the horizontal lines of the building again, and giving it height and dignity. The other variants of the Greek style will illustrate much the same principles in different degrees, and we may trace the value of proportions, and recurring lines, and different degrees of enrichment through the other four orders.

MARBLE CHAIRS, THEATRE OF DIONYSUS, ATHENS.

As designers, then, we can at least learn some very important lessons from lintel architecture generally, and from the Parthenon in particular, and chiefest amongst these are:

1. The value of simplicity of line.

2. The value of recurring and re-echoing lines.

3. The value of ornamental design and treatment of figures in low or high relief as parts of architectural expression

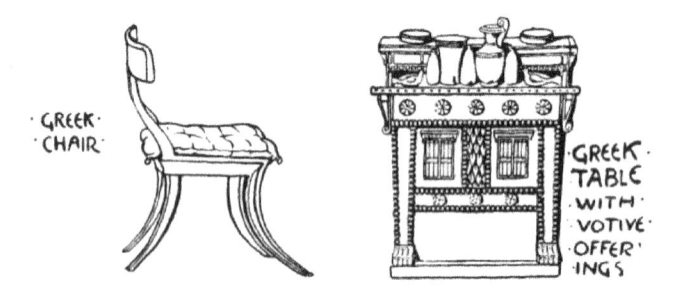

GREEK CHAIR.
GREEK TABLE WITH VOTIVE OFFERINGS.

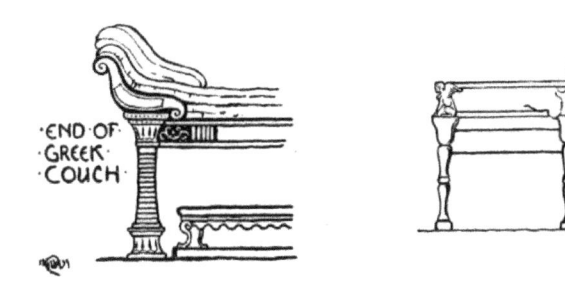

END OF GREEK COUCH.
GREEK LOW-BACKED THRONE.

4. The value of largeness of style in the design and treatment of the groups and figures themselves, both as sculpture pure and simple and as architectural ornament.

When we come to examine the accessories of Greek life, furniture, pottery, dress, we find them all characterized by the same qualities in design as we have just been noting in the architecture; the fundamental architectural feeling seems to pervade them. A simplicity of line, balance, and reserve of ornament distinguishes alike their seats and chairs and tables, caskets, vases and vessels, and the expressive lines of their dresses and draperies falling into the lines of the figure give life and variety, while they contrast with the severity of the architectural lines and planes.

Now, so far we have been considering the architecture of the lintel, and its bearing upon design, and the qualities and principles we may learn from it generally.

With the use of the round arch—invented, it is said, by the Greeks, but always associated with the Romans, who used it—quite different effects come in, with different motives and ideas in design. The Roman architecture, the round arch, fulfils the functions of both construction and ornament, on the same principle of recurrence, or repetition, we have noticed before; as, for instance, in the Colosseum, where the tiers of round arches which support the outer wall of the building serve both the constructive and decorative functions. With the use of the arch the arcade becomes a constructive feature of great decorative value, and takes the place in Roman and Romanesque buildings, with a lighter and more varied effect, of the columned Greek cella. Sunshine, no doubt, had much to do with its use, since a covered arcaded loggia, or porch in front of a building, so frequent in Italy, gave both shelter and coolness. The use of the arch led to vaulting, and to the use of arch mouldings, enrichments, and to the covering the vaults with mosaic and painting, and the vaulting led to the dome, which, again, offered a splendid field for the mosaicist and the painter.

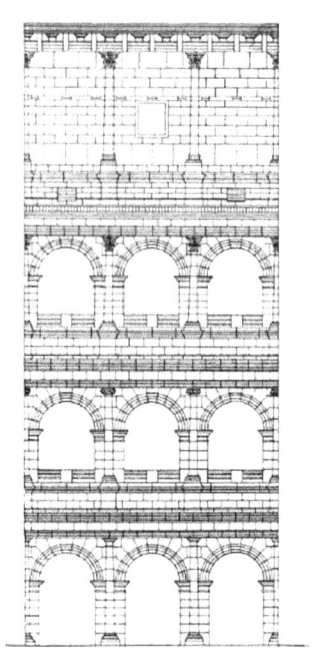

CONSTRUCTIVE & DECORATIVE USE OF ROUND ARCH & PILASTER FLAVIAN AMPHITHEATRE (COLOSSEUM) ROME.

(FERGUSON).

The Romans borrowed all their architectural details from the Greeks, and varied and enriched them, adding many more members to the cornice mouldings, and carving stone garlands upon their friezes, to take the place of the primitive festal ones of leaves which were hung there, as in the relief of the visit of Bacchus to Icarius, a Romano-Greek sculpture in the British Museum.

**HANGING OF THE FESTAL GARLAND,
FROM A GRÆCO ROMAN RELIEF IN THE BRITISH
MUSEUM.**

They (the Romans) fully realized the ornamental value of colonnades and porticoes, and they used the column, varying the orders, and translating them into pilasters freely as decorations on the façades and walls of their buildings, slicing up the peristyles of temples, as it were, for the sake of their ornamental effect, cutting down the columns into pilasters, and placing them, with intervening friezes, one on the top of the other, masking the construction of the real building, a favourite device with the Renascence architects.

USE OF DECORATIVE SCULPTURE IN ROMAN ARCHITECTURE: THE ARCH OF CONSTANTINE.

Roman architecture may be considered really as a transitional style. While its true constructive characteristic is the round arch, every detail of the Greek or Lintel architecture is used both without and with the arch, and in the latter case the column frequently becomes a wall decoration in the shape of a pilaster, as well as the cornice, and is no longer made use of, as in true lintel construction, to support the weight of the roof. In their viaducts and bridges and baths they were great builders with the arch, but, like some modern engineers, when they wanted to beautify they borrowed architectural ornament from the Greeks.

Nothing very fresh was gained for design in these adaptations except a certain heavy richness of detail in the sculptured cornices and friezes, and coffered ceilings. The use of the flat pilaster, however, led to the panelled pilaster with its elegant arabesque, which was afterwards revived and developed with such extraordinary grace and variety by the artists of the Renascence and carried from Italy westward.

With the round arch, too, several important decorative spaces were given to the designer, the spandrel, the panel, the medallion, all of which, with the frieze, may be seen utilized for the decorative sculpture on the arch of Constantine. The decorative use of inscriptions is also a feature in Roman architecture, and the dignity of the form of their capital letters was well adapted to ornamental effect in square masses upon their triumphal arches and along the entablature of their temples.

The Romans, too, brought the domed roof and the mosaic floor into use, and were great in the use of coloured marbles; also stucco and plaster work in interiors, the free and beautiful plaster work found in the tombs on the Latin Way being well known; so that on the whole we owe to them the illustration of the effective use of many beautiful arts, which the Italians have inherited to this day, though it must be said often with more skill than taste.

One might say, generally and ultimately, Roman art exemplified that love of show, and the external signs of power, pomp, splendour, and luxury which became dear as well as fatal to them, as they appear to do to every conquering people, until they are finally enervated and overcome as if by the Nemesis of their own supremacy.

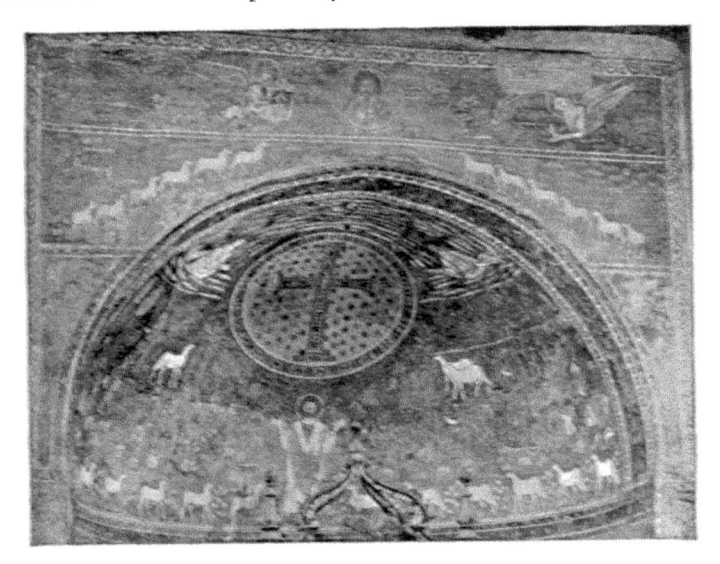

MOSAIC, ST. APOLLINARE IN CLASSE, RAVENNA.

The art of Greece, one may say, on the other hand, at her zenith represented that love of beauty as distinct from ornament, and clearness and severity of thought which will always cling to the country from whence the modern world derives the germ of nearly all its ideas.

But when the seat of the empire was transferred to Constantinople, and Roman art, influenced by Asiatic feeling, and stimulated and elevated by the new faith of Christianity, became transfigured into the solemn splendour of Byzantine art, the architecture of the round arch and the dome and cupola rose to its fullest beauty, and such buildings as St. Sophia at Constantinople, and St. Mark's at Venice, with the churches of Ravenna, mark another great and noble epoch in the arts of design.

Byzantine design, whether in building, in carving, in mosaic, or goldsmiths' work, impresses one with a certain restraint in the midst of its splendour; a certain controlling dignity and reserve appears to be exercised even in the use of the most beautiful materials, as well as in design and the treatment of form.

The mosaics of the Ravenna churches alone are sufficient to exemplify this. The artists seemed fully to realize that the curved surfaces of the dome, the half dome of the apse, or the long flat frieze above the arch columns of the nave of the basilicas, like St. Apollinare in Classe, afforded splendid fields for a splendid material, the cross light from the deep-set windows enriching the effect, and that everything might well be secondary to it. The same principle or feeling is seen in St. Mark's where the architecture is quite simple, the arches and vaulting without mouldings, nothing to interfere with the quiet splendour of the gold or blue fields of mosaic varied with simple typical figures, bold in silhouette, placed frankly upon them, emblems, boldly curving scroll-work, and inscriptions. The execution, too, is as direct and simple as the design. Such design and decoration as this becomes an essential and integral part of the architectural structure and effect.

SKETCH OF PART OF INTERIOR OF DOME, S. MARK'S, VENICE.

MOSAIC OF THE EMPRESS THEODORA, T. VITALE, RAVENNA, SIXTH CENTURY.

Note the way in which the tesseræ are laid (in the head of the Empress Theodora from St. Vitale at Ravenna, for instance). The cube is used as much as possible, but the cubes vary much in size, and are set often with very open joints, the cement lines of the bedding showing quite clearly, and the surface of the work uneven, the tesseræ being worked, of course, from the front and *in situ*, presenting a varied surface of different facets which, catching the light at different angles, give an extraordinary sparkle and richness to the effect as a whole. In the head of Theodora the effect is enhanced by the discs of mother-of-pearl used for the head-dress.

In the laying of the tesseræ, too, note that the system is followed of defining the outlines with rows of cubes, and building up the masses (as in the nimbus) with concentric rows, as a rule, making the lines of the filling tesseræ follow as far as possible the line of the boundary tesseræ. This, of course, would naturally result as the simplest and most convenient, as well as most expressive, method of laying tesseræ, in defining form by means of small cubes, and is one of the conditions of the work, and when, as in these mosaics, so far from being refined away, or concealed, or any attempt being made (as in later times) to imitate painting, these conditions are boldly and frankly acknowledged, we see how its peculiar beauty, character, and the quality of its ornamental effect depends upon these very conditions.

This principle will be found to hold good and true throughout all art. Directly, from a false idea of refinement, or with the object of displaying mechanical skill, the craftsman is induced to try to conceal the fundamental conditions of his craft, and to make it ape the qualities of some totally different sort of work, he ceases to be an artist, at all events. The true artist in any material is he who in acknowledging its conditions and limitations finds in them sources and opportunities of new beauty, and in being faithful to those conditions makes them subserve his invention.

After the decorative splendour of the Byzantine architecture, the Norman work left in our own land seems comparatively simple and plain as time has left it, but its remains show its Roman descent in the doorway and porch of many a quiet village church, as well as on a greater scale in so many of our cathedrals, which often illustrate, in a remarkable way, the transition or growth of one style out of another, the new evolved from the old.

At Canterbury, for instance, one reads the signs which mark the transformation of the Norman building into the Gothic. The first church founded by St. Augustine was Saxon. This was enlarged by Otho (938) as a basilica. This again was ruined by the Danes (1013). The Norman part of the present building was constructed by Bishop Lanfranc (1070), on to which was grafted, as it were, the thirteenth, fourteenth, and fifteenth century Gothic which distinguish it.

There is a tower on the south side of the transept known as Anselm's Tower (from Bishop Anselm, one of the Norman builders), and on the lower part runs an arcading of interlacing round arches, the tower itself being richly arcaded in several stories in round arches. But this lower band shows the period of transition, from the use of the round arch, to the pointed—the pointed lancet arches being formed by the interlacing of the round, so that we have here the actual birth of *the pointed arch* (at least, as a decorative feature), which leads us to our next typical division and characteristic epoch of architectural style.

ANSELM'S TOWER, CANTERBURY.

We need not go out of our own country to find abundant illustrations of typical forms of pointed architecture. Almost any village church will give us the main features—the characteristic plan of nave and chancel, curiously following the plan of the ancient Roman basilica—the public hall and law court in one, and perpetuating for us the type of ancient dwelling or hall which may be said to have prevailed from the time of Homer to the end of the Middle Ages, varying chiefly in external features and architectural detail.

The severe lancet arch is characteristic of the first phase of the Gothic, which gradually grew out of the severer Norman. The *gable* took a higher pitch, and to support the weight and thrust of *towers* and *spires*, *buttresses* were used, and these became, also, a striking and characteristic feature of the pointed arch, which completed in the thirteenth century the period of its first development.

Lancet arch, high-pitched gable, buttress (plain and pinnacled), spired and pinnacled tower—these are the leading constructive exterior characteristics, the carved work, somewhat restrained, and chiefly manifested in peculiar foliation of the capitals and corbels, and in the hollows of arch mouldings in rows of sharp cut dog teeth.

In the interior clustered shafts took the place of the solid round Norman piers, rising, as we see in our cathedral naves, to support lofty vaulted roofs, the ribs moulded and covered at their intersections by carved bosses.

Again we may note the principle of recurring lines which repeat and emphasize the form of the arched openings and the structural lines of the vaulting in the mouldings. This recurrence gives that effect of extraordinary grace and lightness combined with structural strength which is so striking a characteristic of thirteenth century Gothic work, and of which there is no finer example than the nave of Westminster Abbey.

TRANSITIONAL ARCADE, SOUTH TRANSEPT, CANTERBURY.

TYPICAL FORMS OF ARCHES:

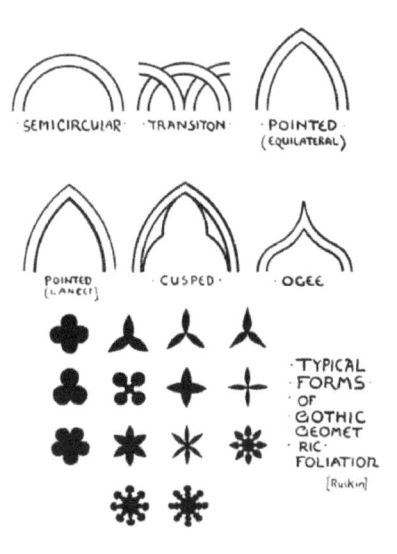

TYPICAL FORMS OF GOTHIC GEOMETRIC FOLIATION.

[Ruskin].

WESTMINSTER ABBEY: THE NAVE, LOOKING EAST.

We noted that the Greeks used the interstices of their construction for their chief decoration, their figure sculpture, and to some extent the same plan is followed in Gothic architecture, where we find the tympanums of doors, the spandrels of arcades (as in the Chapter House at Salisbury or the angel choir at Lincoln), and canopied niches (as at Wells), used for figure sculpture; but, at the same time, the *structural features themselves are emphasized* by ornament to a far greater extent, as in caps, arch mouldings, the junctions of the vaulting, and the like; and increasingly so in the succeeding Decorated and Perpendicular periods, until we get vaulted roofs of fan tracery like those of King's College Chapel at Cambridge, or Henry VII.'s Chapel at Westminster.

But if we may say that the chief decorative glory of Greek architecture was its figure sculpture, as mosaic was of the Byzantine churches, so we may say that the traceried window, filled with stained and leaded glass, became the chief decorative glory of Gothic architecture.

Unhappily great quantities of glass have disappeared from our cathedrals and churches, from one cause or another, but from the relics that remain we may form some idea of the splendour and quality of the old glass.

The famous windows of the south transept at York Minster, called "The Five Sisters," are good examples of the severer earlier style of pattern and colour, consisting of fine scroll-work and geometric forms, in which hatched grisaille patterns are heightened by bright points and lines of colour.

WEST FRONT OF WELLS CATHEDRAL.

Thirteenth century glass, where figures are used, is characterized by the smallness of their scale in proportion to the window, and traces of

Byzantine tradition in their drawing, intricate design, and deep and vivid colouring, the work being composed of small pieces of glass leaded together; the effect of the jewel-like depth and quality of the colour—deep crimsons, blues, and greens being much used—being increased by the close network of leading.

As windows, in the course of the evolution of the Gothic style, were made broader, or rather, the window opening proper from wall to wall being greatly increased in width and height, they were supported and divided into panels or lights by elaborate stone tracery, a tracery which becomes almost as distinct a province of design as the design of the glass itself—distinct from, yet in close relationship to the architecture of the building. The comparative slight divisions of the tracery, however, gave more scope to the stained glass designer, who shows very emphatic architectural influence in the elaborate canopies which surmount the figures occupying the separate lights of the windows from the thirteenth to the end of the fifteenth centuries, as well as in the general vertical arrangement of the lines of their composition. He gradually increased the scale of his figures and gave more breadth to his design, and brought it more into relation with the art of the painter and the sculptor, at the same time acknowledging with them, in the disposition of his figures in the space, and the disposition of the draperies and accessories, that architectural influence under which the artist and craftsman of the Middle Ages worked with extraordinary freedom and fertility of invention, and yet in perfect harmony[2]—a sign of that fraternal co-operation and the effect of the formation of men into brotherhoods and guilds, which, coming in with the adoption of Christianity and the organization of the Church, remained through all the turbulence and strife of the time the great social force of the Middle Ages.

WESTMINSTER ABBEY, FAN TRACERY IN HENRY VII.'S CHAPEL, FIFTEENTH CENTURY.

It seems to me if we wish to realize the ideal of a great and harmonious art, which shall be capable of expressing the best that is in us: if we desire again to raise great architectural monuments, religious, municipal, or commemorative, we shall have to learn the great lesson of unity through fraternal co-operation and sympathy, the particular work of each, however individual and free in artistic expression, falling naturally into its due place in a harmonious scheme. Let us cultivate our technical skill and knowledge to the utmost, but let us not neglect our imagination, sense of beauty, and sympathy, or else we shall have nothing to express.

Through the thirteenth century onwards to the fifteenth Gothic architecture continued to develop, to pass through new phases, to take new forms, a living and growing style moving with the wants and ideals of men.

After the Early English comes the Decorated period, in which the mouldings and foliation become fuller, broader, and more ornate. To contrast decorated foliation and ornament with the earlier work, is like comparing the opening flower with the bud. The ogee arch was invented, the crockets of the pinnacles and canopies grew and increased and became finer in form, the finials larger and more varied. The carved canopies and tabernacle work grew richer and more intricate. The foliage followed nature more closely. The figure subjects of the carver were more freely treated, and dealt oftener with common life, with phantasy, or humour. The effigies of knight and lady, or priest, became more and more like portraits in stone or alabaster, the details of their dresses more rich, delicate, and beautiful. The maker of brasses showed a freer and more masterly hand, and greater sense of ornamental effect in the spacing and treatment of his figures. The work of the miniaturist and the scribe grew more and more delicate and exquisite in form, colour, and invention. The stained glass worker increased the scale of his figures, and varied the quality and treatment of his colours. The glazier invented new lead patterns; the wood carver revelled in stall work, screens, and misereres. The recessed and canopied tomb enriched the chantries of churches and cathedrals.

THE FIVE SISTERS OF YORK THIRTEENTH CENTURY.

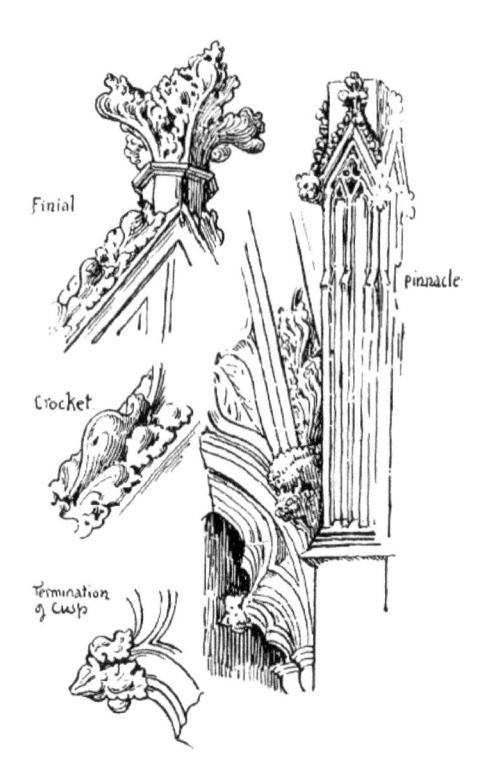

DETAILS OF TOMB WINCHELSEA CH. 1303.

Finial.
Pinnacle.
Crocket.
Termination of Cusp.

FOURTEENTH CENTURY CANOPIED TOMB, WINCHELSEA CHURCH.

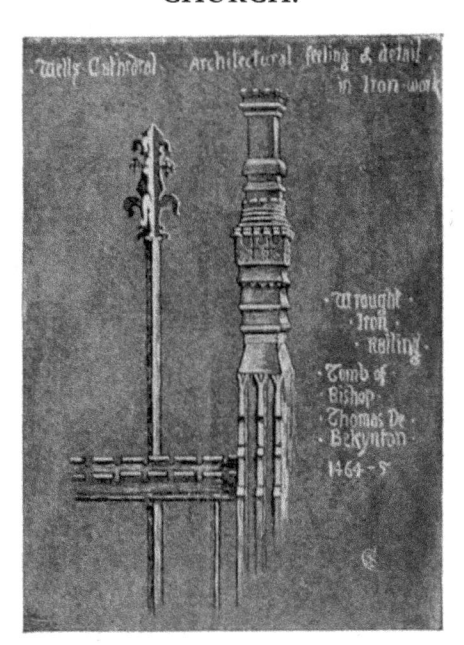

Wells Cathedral Architectural feeling & detail in iron work.

Wrought-Iron Railing.
Tomb of Bishop Thomas De Bekynton 1464-5.

Beauty and invention of extraordinary fertility and richness characterized every form of art and handicraft associated with Gothic architecture. We can trace in each variety the architectural influence in every department of work. In some instances reproduction of actual architectural details and characteristics, as, for instance, when the wrought-iron railing of a bishop's tomb (at Wells Cathedral, 1464-5) reproduced the battlement, buttress and pinnacle as motives, giving them, however, a free and fanciful rendering suited to the material.

DRESSOIR OR SIDE BOARD 15th CENT. FRENCH

(from L. Roger Milès)

CANOPIED SEAT FRENCH 15th CENT.

Abundant instances may be found of the fanciful treatment of architectural forms in furniture, textiles, in painting and carving, and metal work—the canopies over the heads of figures in stained glass, and inclosing figures upon brasses, are instances—shrines and caskets in the form of arcaded, and buttressed and pinnacled buildings, seats and chairs with canopied or arched backs, carved bench ends with "poppy head" finials and arched and foliated panels, censers in the form of shrines. The large gold brocaded stuffs used as hangings or coverings, and represented in miniatures and pictures of the period. Very beautiful specimens are to be seen in the pictures of Van Eyck and Memling for instance.

CARVED BENCH-ENDS, DENNINGTON CHURCH, SUFFOLK.

In all these things we find a re-echo, as it were, of the prevailing foliated forms of Gothic architecture, repeated through endless variations, the controlling and harmonizing element throughout the design work of the Gothic periods, the form by which all seem to be harmonized and related, as the branches are related to the main stem, and as the plan of the tree may be found in the veining of the leaf.

The fourteenth century saw the development of a new phase of Gothic called Perpendicular. It is found united with the Early English and Decorated, as well as Norman, in nearly all our cathedrals.

BROCADE HANGING, FROM THE ANNUNCIATION, BY MEMLING.

At St. David's, for instance, there is a remarkable instance of a late Perpendicular timber roof, richly moulded and carved, with pendants, covering a Norman nave of 1180. Yet the effect is fine, and one feels glad that the restoring architect could find no authority for a Norman stone vaulting, otherwise we might have lost the rich timber roof for a modern idea of a supposititious Norman vault. The sketch (from the south side of the choir at Canterbury, p. 45), too, shows how harmoniously structural lines of different periods compose.

The chief characteristics of the late period of Gothic (Perpendicular) are a lower pitched arch, an elongated shaft, many clustered; caps and bases angular; ribs of vaulting richly moulded, or the vault covered with fan-like foliation in late examples, as in Henry VII.'s Chapel. Pinnacles begin to take the cupular form, details become smaller, windows grow larger and are transversely divided by transoms or horizontal bars of stone, connecting and solidifying the many vertical mullions.

ST. DAVID'S CATHEDRAL.

A certain refinement of detail and line with a feeling for emphatic horizontals and verticals comes in; and this feeling may be the indication of a reaction, as if the constructive and imaginative faculties of man were beginning to prepare for the next great change that was soon to sweep over the art of Europe.

STRUCTURAL LINES OF DIFFERENT PERIODS IN HARMONIOUS COMBINATION, CANTERBURY CATHEDRAL.

It might be said that gradually from that time architecture, as the supreme organic and controlling influence in the arts of design, gave up her prerogative of leadership, and since has rather been on the whole displaced in artistic interest by the other arts; or rather, with the change of the principle of organic growth out of use and constructive necessity in architecture for those of classical authority, archæology, or learned eclecticism, the different arts, more especially painting, began an independent existence, and, with the other arts of design, may be said to have been more individualized and less and less related both to them and to architecture ever since, reaching the extremest points of divergence perhaps in our own days.

It seems to me that, on the whole, there can be little doubt that architecture and the arts of design generally have suffered in consequence; and to bring them back to healthy and harmonious activity we must try to re-unite them all again upon the old basis.

I will terminate here my short sketch of architectural style and its influence, not attempting now to follow it in its later changes and adaptations to the increased complexities of human existence. My purpose has been rather to dwell upon the organic and typical forms of architecture, in my endeavour to trace the relationship between it and the art of design generally.

That relationship appears to me to consist chiefly in *the control of constructive line and form*, which all design, surface or otherwise, in association with any form of architecture is bound of necessity to acknowledge as a fundamental condition of fitness and harmony. Those essential properties of the expression of line, as they now seem, which give meaning and purpose to all design, appear to be derived straight from constructive necessities and the inseparable association of ideas with which they are connected; as, for instance, the idea of secure rest and repose conveyed by horizontal lines, or the sense of support and rigidity suggested by vertical ones may be directly traced to association with the fundamental principles of architectural structure, to the lintel and its support, to the laying of stone upon stone, and with this clue we might trace the expression of line through its many variations.

CHAPTER II.—OF THE UTILITY BASIS AND INFLUENCE

NEXT to the architectural basis influence in design, and, indeed, hardly separable from it, being another side of the constructive, adaptive art, we may fitly take the Utility Basis and influence.

This may be considered in two ways:

> (1) In its effect upon pattern design and architectural ornament through primitive structural necessities.
>
> (2) In its effect upon structural form and ornamental treatment arising out of, or suggested by, functional use.

(1) It is a curious thing that we should find the primitive ornamental motives bound up with the primitive structures and fabrics of pure utility and necessity, but such would appear to be the case.

The plaiting of rushes to make a mat was probably one of the earliest industrial occupations, and the chequer one of the most primitive and universal of patterns. If we look at the surface effect of the necessity of the construction, the crossing of one equal set of fibres by another set at right angles, with the interlacement, a series of squares are produced, which alternate in tint if the colour of one set is darker than the sets which cross it (see illustration). Emphasize this contrast and we get our chequer, or chessboard pattern, which, either as a pattern complete in itself, as in plaids and tartans, or as a plan, or effect motive in designing is, as I have said, perhaps the most universal and imperishable of all patterns, being found in association with the design of all periods, and still surviving in constant use among designers.

MATTING.

Let us follow the primitive rush mat a little further, however. As it lay on the primitive tent or hut floor its edges would take the sort of form shown on the following page. In ancient Assyrian, Egyptian, Persian, and Greek architecture we constantly find carved patterns used as borderings and figures, of the type given in the Assyrian example. Now, comparing this with the primitive matting, the suggestion is very strong of the probability of derivation of motive of patterns of this type from the same constructive source originally. In some instances, as on the enamelled tile from Assyria, the border reverses itself, but with the Greeks it finally took the upright direction, as in the Anthemion or honeysuckle border forms; but, however afterwards varied and enriched by floral form, its structural origin in plaited work is always to be traced, and it seems to gain from it a certain strength and adaptability.

PRIMITIVE RUSH MAT AND ASSYRIAN BORDER.

ASSYRIAN INCISED BORDER.

Another type of ornament may be traced to the constructive necessities of wattle and wicker work, so much used by primitive man in the structure of his dwellings, and in primitive objects of use and service.

ASSYRIAN ENAMELLED TILE.

The various forms of volute, or spiral, and guilloche ornament, so much used by the ancients—Assyrian, Egyptian, and Greek—may be compared, in their structure and arrangement of line, with the form taken by the withy, or cord twisted around the upright canes or staves of a wattled fence, as seen in horizontal section. The primitive wattled structure gives the plans of these patterns. It certainly appears to account for their origin in a remarkably complete way.

GREEK ANTHEMION ORNAMENT.

WATTLED FENCE.

It is possible that another source which may have contributed to the evolution of the Greek spiral or volute was metal in the form of the thin beaten plates with which the primitive Greeks covered parts of their interior walls; but these were later times, and it is also possible that the primitive metal worker took his motive from the wattling too.

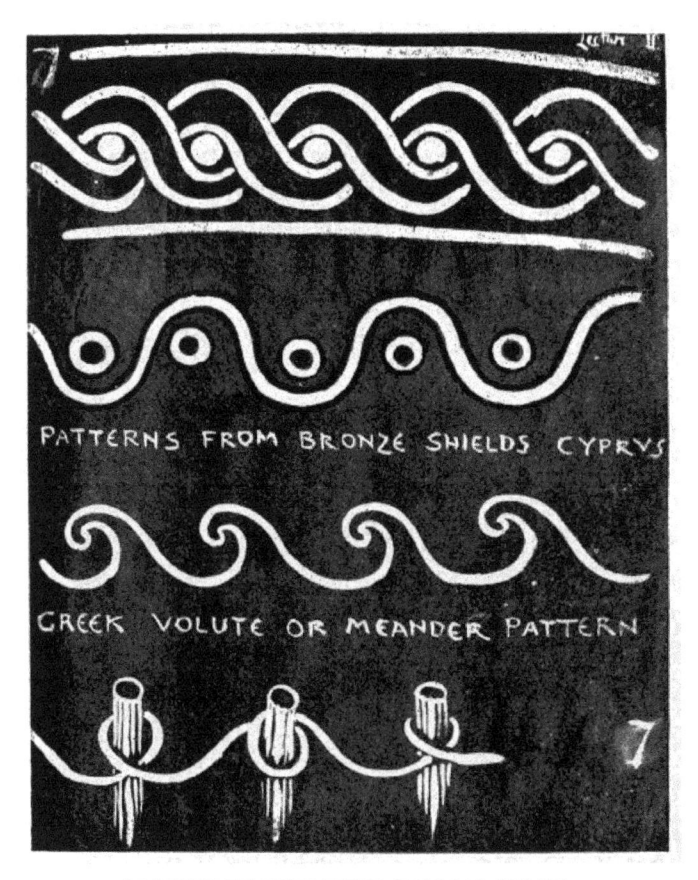

ANCIENT VOLUTE ORNAMENT.

PATTERNS FROM BRONZE SHIELDS CYPRUS.
GREEK VOLUTE OR MEANDER PATTERN.

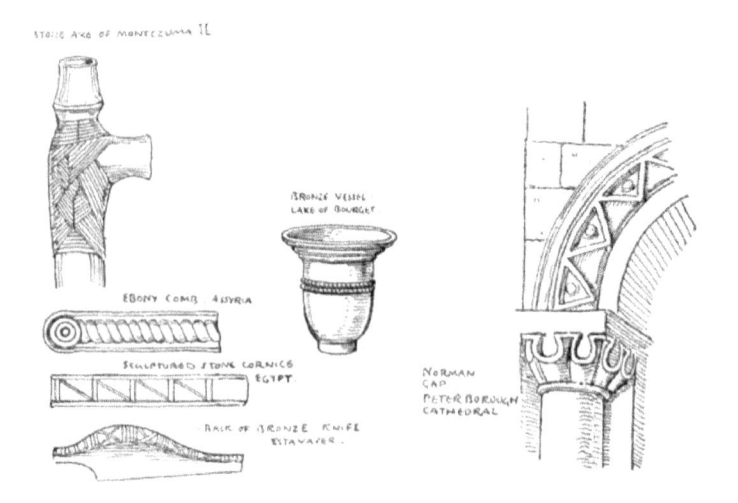

TYPES OF DECORATION DERIVED FROM THONGING.

STONE AXE OF MONTEZUMA II.
BRONZE VESSEL, LAKE OF BOURGET.
EBONY COMB, ASSYRIA.
SCULPTURED STONE CORNICE, EGYPT.
NORMAN CAP, PETERBOROUGH CATHEDRAL.
BACK OF BRONZE KNIFE ESTAVAYER.

Before metal was used, or nails or joinery were known, the method of fastening two things together, such as the blade of a stone axe or hammer and its handle, was by thonging or tying them firmly together by strips of leather or thongs, and to this source again we might trace other types of pattern motives of very wide prevalence. In the first instances the thonging was imitated in metal-work when no longer used in the construction by way of ornament, as in various bronze implements existing; but later, starting from the tying and thonging motive, we get all sorts of variations, as in the zigzag of Norman arch mouldings, and in the earlier Celtic knotted work, which seemed partly a re-echo of some types of Eastern and classic ornament, unless we regard it as independently derived, like them, from primitive structure. It seems to make itself felt again in a new variety in the strap-work of our Elizabethan period, in which the ornament apparently was a new blend of Gothic with classical details, with an infusion of oriental or Moorish feeling, filtered through Italy and Spain.

FRIEZE (TEMPLE OF THE SIBYL TIVOLI).

YOKE OF OXEN, CARRARA.

As an instance of architectural ornament, the motive of which seems taken from a piece of common every-day usage, we may note the frieze of the Roman circular Temple of the Sibyl at Tivoli, which is composed of the heads of oxen, alternating with, and connected by, the curves of pendent floral garlands. To this day in Italy almost anywhere one may see this motive suggested by the appearance of the country ox wagon as it approaches along the road—the front view of the two oxen heads, with the level yoke across their necks, and the pendent connecting ropes hanging between.

It is probable, however, that whatever its origin, its suggestion was sacrificial, since the ox decked with garlands constantly figures in classical sculpture led before the altar to be slain, and this circumstance may equally have given rise to the sculptor's motive, just as we saw that the custom of decking the cornice of the Greek house with garlands suggested its perpetuation in stone carving by the classical architects.

It will be noted that those primitive sources to which we may trace motives in ornamental design, however, afterwards developed on purely ornamental lines, and because of their ornamental value, all of them have their beginnings in actual use and service, in physical and constructive necessity, and that they are closely associated with the form and character of the dwellings and temples of man.

(2) Turning now to the second division of our subject to consider "the effects upon form and treatment of surface arising out of, or suggested by, functional use," we shall still have to keep close to the dwelling, and constantly to remember the ever present architectural influence with the consideration of which we set out.

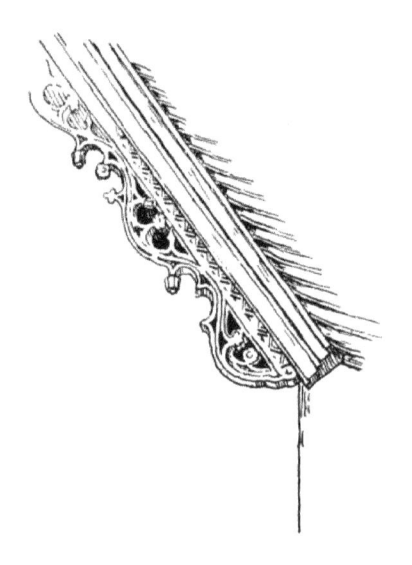

BARGE-BOARD, IGHTHAM MOTE HOUSE.

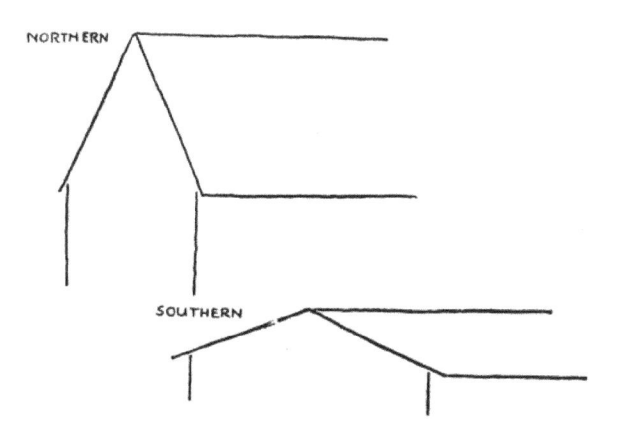

TYPE OF GABLES:

NORTHERN.
SOUTHERN.

The angle of the pitch of the roof in buildings, for instance, which is so marked a characteristic in the different types of architecture, was originally determined by the necessities of climate. One might say broadly that the acute, high-pitched Gothic roof means snow or bad weather, while the low-pitched classic roof means sunshine for the most part; or we might say that the one typified winter and the other summer. A house must still be built mainly for one or the other, though by ingenuity and careful consideration of the points of the compass in choosing the site and planning, in the rare instances where free choice is still possible, something may be, and *has* been attempted, to fit all seasons; and it is this careful consideration of such points in our ancient buildings—say the old English manor houses, built to dwell in and to last—which gives that sense of homelike comfort and pleasure to the eye, perhaps, quite as much as the interest of their ornamental detail. A sunny garden terrace or arcaded front to the south to catch the winter sun—cool and shady rooms to the north for the summer—a sheltered porch to protect the guest against the weather. Such contrivances as these show that thought has been spent and care taken in the planning and building; that the builder or designer has been influenced by considerations of true utility—not in the bald and more modern sense of mere money or time saving appliance, but the truer economy of making a house *livable*. Here is a sketch of one of those old stone halls or manor houses of Derbyshire of the seventeenth century (Hazelford Hall), charmingly placed upon a hillside, so as to fit into or become part of the landscape, while it is really planned to live comfortably in, with due regard to the variation of the seasons and the winds. The living rooms face south and west.

Houses nowadays seem more built to sell than to live in (at least permanently), since I notice that often even when people build a house for themselves they constantly want to let it to somebody else. I should think that the gipsy van would suit modern habits exceedingly well. It would be more picturesque than "a brick box with a slate lid," to which most of us are committed, and probably much less expensive in the long run. The only thing required to make it practicable on any scale is a trifling alteration in the land laws.

The origin of mouldings in architecture, as their use in the capacity of dripstones declares, was to serve a purely useful purpose—the alternating concavity and convexity of the members which generally characterize them affording escapement for the rain water, and keeping it away from the windows and doors.

HAZELFORD HALL, DERBYSHIRE.

To give a simple illustration of the principle. If the sill of a window, for instance, be left rectangular and perfectly level, the water would be likely to run inward through the window, or perhaps into the wall, but if sloped on the upper surface and hollowed beneath, the water would tend to drop from the under outer edge clear of both window and wall.

SECTION TO SHOW ACTION OF RAIN ON WINDOW SILLS: (1)PLAIN & MOULDED(2).

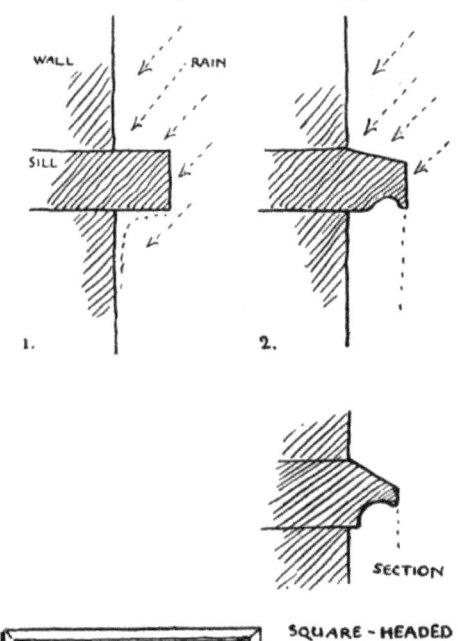

SECTION.
SQUARE-HEADED DRIPSTONE.

This necessity led to motives in design and ornamental effect, and mouldings became valuable parts of æsthetic expression in architecture, affording means of emphasis, of giving the effect of receding planes, and of using the important principle of recurring lines to which I called attention in the first chapter.

The barge-board, too, so picturesque a feature in old timbered houses, had the same useful purpose to subserve in keeping the weather from injuring roof and wall.

Staircases with the necessary handrail, again, have led to beautiful form in design, not only in the planning of the staircase itself, which is so important a feature in every house, but in the interesting and varied design in the balusters supporting the handrail, and in newel heads, etc.

THE TOWERS OF SAN GIMIGNANO.

THE TOWERS OF SAN GIMIGNANO.

Towers and church steeples, which form such important and picturesque features in architectural (and, one might add, landscape) design, owed their existence, in the first place, to the necessities of watch, guard, and defence, and probably also means of communication by signals.

To the mediæval city, which, as it is now being realized, was a highly organized arrangement for mutual aid and defence, towers were of great importance both for watch and defence. They served as strong buttresses and vantage posts placed at intervals along the inclosing city wall, and flanking the gateways. The boldness and grace of design in some mediæval towers is very notable. Those of Siena, for instance, and that town of towers, San Gimignano, of which I give a rough sketch to show the effect from a distance of the clustering towers, like a crown upon the hill top; above all, perhaps, is the famous tower of the Signoria or Palazzo Vecchio, the old city hall of Florence (thirteenth century). The Belfry of Bruges (thirteenth century), too, is another fine instance of boldness and grace of design. It had formerly a spire, which is shown in a sixteenth century picture, the background of a portrait by Pourbus, a Flemish painter, but the spire was twice destroyed by fire, and was not renewed a third time. But even as it stands the belfry is very striking, and, while it commands a vast prospect of the country round, it is also conspicuous all over the town, and a landmark to the flat country round about.

The towers of our own ancient village churches are generally battlemented, and the square ones often have a corner turret to give a more commanding view; and this again gives variety, and is a very picturesque feature. The battlements themselves (though intended for use in defence) are extremely ornamental features, and give relief and lightness to the parapet. In later

Gothic times they were frequently fancifully pieced and filled with ornament, as on Magdalen Tower at Oxford. Their decorative value was perceived by the wood carver of the Gothic times, and they are constantly introduced in tabernacle work, screens, and furniture, where their use is purely decorative.

TOWER OF PALAZZO VECCHIO, FLORENCE.

Chimneys, again, afford an instance of a purely useful and serviceable object lending itself to ornamental treatment and becoming important as parts of the design of a building.

The first chimney in England is said to be the one existing in the Norman house at Christchurch, Hampshire. The common practice was to have the fireplace in the centre of the hall and let the smoke escape by a louvre in the roof, as may still be seen in the hall at Penshurst Place in Kent (fourteenth century); but in later times, especially in the Tudor period, the chimneys of brick are often found full of invention and variety in design, and extremely rich in effect. I give sketches of some characteristic examples at Framlingham Castle and Leigh's Priory.

TOWER WITH CORNER TURRET, AXMOUTH CHURCH, DEVON.

The fine old brick chimney stacks one finds among the old farmsteads of Essex it is supposed were built first and then the half-timbered house built around the brick stack.

CUT BRICK CHIMNEYS, LEIGH'S PRIORY, ESSEX.

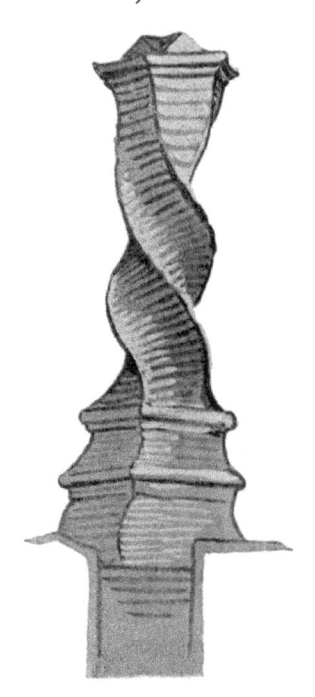

BRICK CHIMNEY, FRAMLINGHAM CASTLE.

Other useful things connected with the fireside and the chimney corner, which are remarkable for their adaptability in ornamental design, are the iron fire-dogs used to support the burning logs. We find them in great variety of shape and treatment, while their main or necessary lines remain the same. It is the standard or upright front part which affords a field for the inventive craftsman and designer. The fire-irons, too, are again purely useful in their object, but have become highly graceful and elegant in some of their forms.

The iron grate back (notably those of old Sussex), placed at the back of the fire against the chimney to protect the brick-work and radiate the heat, had again a purely useful function, but it has been the object of a great deal of fine and rich decorative design, chiefly of a heraldic or emblematic character, and many old examples exist. Cast iron has in modern times acquired a bad name (artistically speaking), but this is owing to its misapplication, as in railings or grills, where it endeavours to usurp the place of wrought iron. In a flat panel or plain surface, such as a grate back affords, however, cast iron has a singularly good effect, and renders bold designs well. There are some fine heraldic grate backs in cast iron to be seen at Cheetham's Hospital, perhaps the most interesting building in the City of Manchester.

CAST-IRON FIRE-DOG, ST. NICHOLAS HOSPITAL, CANTERBURY.

I give a sketch of a quaint cast-iron chimney back of Gothic design from Bruges. At the Museum at the old Rath Haus there is a very good collection of examples. Somehow, with the modern, or rather mid-Victorian iron register fireplace all beauty and interest of design is lost. Though it should be remembered that a really fine artist and designer like Alfred Stevens spent his talent upon such things.

The conception of the thing, however, seems joyless and ugly, and in most surviving examples the ornament in endeavouring to be elegant becomes frittered and mean; and as to sheet-iron stoves they seem to be under a ban of hideousness, which seems sad when one recalls the charming and cheerful earthenware stoves of Germany of Gothic and Renascence times, full of colour and invention. The revived use of tiled chimney, and recessed and basket grates, has done much to restore cheerfulness to our hearths.

CAST-IRON GRATE BACK.

Before we leave the chimney corner I might mention another bit of metal, important before the days of kitchen ranges as the chief cooking apparatus, I mean the iron crane that is sometimes found still suspended in the wide chimneys of old farmhouses, made of wrought iron, twisted and curled, and with bright bosses of steel upon it, and great in hooks and hinges. Here is a sketch of a typical example in an Essex farmhouse.

FIREPLACE WITH WROUGHT IRON CRANE
CHURCH FARM HEMPSTEAD ESSEX

FIREPLACE WITH WROUGHT IRON CRANE, CHURCH FARM, HEMPSTEAD, ESSEX.

Considerations of use, again, very evidently control design in lamps and candlesticks. A lamp necessitates: (1) *a reservoir for the oil*, and (2) *a neck and mouth* to hold the wick, and (3) *a firm and steady stand*. All these requisites are combined, with addition of handle, in the oldest and simplest form of lamp—the portable antique lamp to be carried in the hand. The reservoir is there, though small, and needing re-filling from a larger vessel (as was the case in the parable of the ten virgins).

These lamps were often placed upon the top of slender fluted tripod stands, to give light in the house, or hung in clusters by chains from a branched stand like a tree. A combination of many of the characteristics of the antique lamp is found in the comparatively modern brass Roman lamp (now called antique, but till within a few years, and I believe still, commonly used by the people): we have the small reservoir, with four necks for the wicks, closely resembling in form the antique hand lamps. This is pierced by the shaft of the stand, which finishes in a ring handle at the top and terminates in a broad moulded stand, so that the lamp can be used for carrying or standing with equal facility. The little implements for trimming, snuffing, and extinguishing are suspended by small chains from the neck of the standard and add to the ornamental effect. Each part is made separately and screws together.

With the modern powerful lamps of mineral oil and circular wicks, much larger reservoirs are required, and modern lamps have tended to take the urn shape owing to this necessity, and they lose in beauty of line generally as they gain in body (much like people). A satisfactory type has been introduced by Mr. W. A. S. Benson, of copper, with a copper fan-like shade, which is generally a difficulty with a modern lamp; and the glasses also, while necessary, complicate the design and cannot be said to add to the beauty, as a rule. (See Illustration, p. 77.)

However, a lamp design can never get away from the primitive triple conditions of lamp structure with which we saw in its earliest form *reservoir, neck for the wick*, and *stand*—possibly handle—but within these demands of utility there is scope for very great variations, and unlimited taste and invention.

CANDLESTICKS.

The candlestick, with which the hand lamp has something in common, is, however, quite distinct in character, seeing that it is formed to hold the combustible part in a solid, instead of a liquid form. Its requirements, therefore, are a firm stand (like the lamp), a reasonable height, on which to raise the light, another to hold the candle, and something to catch the melting grease.

These conditions are satisfied in the form of the antique brass candlestick, but still better in the older Gothic form, or the church candlestick, which has a spike on which to hold the candle, instead of a hollow. A candlestick, therefore, should be true to its name and remain a stick, or moulded tubular column, though capable of development into the candelabrum, throwing out branches for extra lights from the central stem; a suggestive form, if sufficiently restrained, designed with taste.

The ancient hanging brass candelabra of the sixteenth, seventeenth, and eighteenth centuries, or earlier, are very good in form as well as practical. There is a fine Gothic one in Van Eyck's picture in the National Gallery, "Jan Arnolfini and his Wife."

I have a good example of the later type—a German one. The stem is surrounded by the double eagle, and there are several tiers of mouldings, the larger ones being flat, and cut into notches at the edge to serve as sockets to receive the corresponding part of the branch, which fits on to them and supports the candles. These are arranged in two tiers of six lights each, and between each light occurs a little ornamental branch or finial, the whole being detachable from the hanging stem terminating in a brass sphere which keeps it straight and steady. It is a fine example of good, simple, and practicable design, which should always unite necessity and utility with beauty.

CHANDELIER OF BRASS, GERMAN 17th CENTURY.

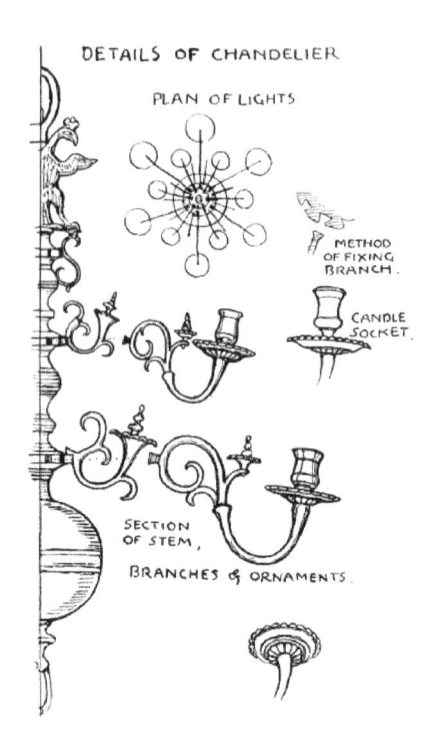

DETAILS OF CHANDELIER:

PLAN OF LIGHTS.
METHOD OF FIXING BRANCH.
CANDLE SOCKET.
SECTION OF STEM, BRANCHES & ORNAMENTS.

For carrying about, a candlestick needs the addition of a broad dish-like stand and handle, while the stick itself is kept low; hardly so attractive a form as the stationary columnar table candlestick, and yet having decided character and purpose of its own.

Those old-fashioned and most picturesque companions of candlesticks, the snuffers, are often very beautiful in design, and it seems to me that, however "improved," the wicks of modern candles still require some attention from them.

The necessity of protecting light affords in lanterns opportunities for the inventive adaptability of the designer in glass and metal.

I met with a very pretty and original motive in a German museum (at Lindau) which was hexagonal in form, pieces of glass fitted together by leads forming a globe-like body to hold the light, and terminating above in a neck, from which it hung to a bracket by a ring. It was furnished with a tripod stand in iron, so that it could be taken down and made to stand if needed.

There is plenty of room for invention in lanterns, and it seems a pity that our street lamp, which is practically a standard lantern, should remain so extremely prosaic, when it is a design so constantly repeated. It is not so much the plainness, since one needs no extraneous ornament if the purpose is well served by a structure of good lines. The necessity of cleaning the glass is probably a hindrance to much variety of form in the present state of things, and then, too, the electric light is coming into general use, bringing with it an entirely fresh set of conditions, so that before we get our ideal gas-lamp the necessity for it will probably have disappeared altogether, so to speak.

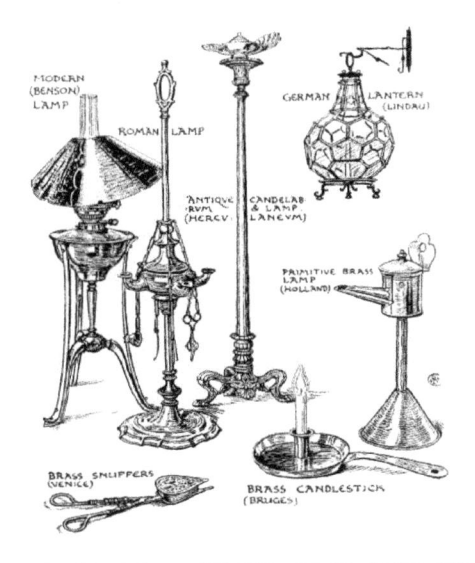

LAMPS, CANDLESTICK, AND SNUFFERS.

MODERN (BENSON) LAMP.
GERMAN LANTERN
(LINDAU).
ROMAN LAMP.
ANTIQUE CANDELABRUM & LAMP
(HERCULANEUM).
PRIMITIVE BRASS LAMP
(HOLLAND).
BRASS SNUFFERS
(VENICE).
BRASS CANDLESTICK
(BRUGES).

The idea of suspension and absence of rigidity or weight associated with electric lighting ought, one would think, to be suggestive to designers, but we don't seem yet to have quite shaken off the conditions of gas tubing on the one hand, or to have got much beyond the somewhat well-worn idea of bell-flowers bursting into incandescence on the other. One almost prefers the naked simplicity of the little pear-shaped glasses, with their incandescent twist of thread suspended at the end of the covered wires, to the flamboyant excesses in brass and copper electric fitting sometimes seen.

One might go on through the whole range of objects of domestic use, and multiply instances of beauty and designing invention applied to the humblest utensil, implement, or accessory, and suggested by the characteristic features stamped upon its form by the necessities and demands of daily use, which must never be lost sight of by the artist. Not a single thing that we touch or use but has had an enormous amount of human thought and ingenuity brought to bear upon it, which has determined its form as we see it, and which is constantly modifying form and material and character.

The present modifying influences, the direction in which human ingenuity mostly seems to work is in the time-saving, cost-saving, labour-saving direction, or would-be so, and under this influence designs of articles or objects of pure utility have a tendency to become very prosaic—or, perhaps, vulgarly assertive. It is the commercial instinct, no doubt, which is satisfied if a knife *is* a knife and will cut, or at any rate will sell, and puts no romance into either blade or handle. The old curved blades have disappeared, and only the silver knife receives any ornament, and that generally of a very uninteresting type. This prosaic tendency represents the mechanical side of the utility influence, which only reaches beauty, if beauty of line merely, by necessity of use; though under what I should term *the short-cut inspiration* beauty is generally entirely out of the question. This is to be deplored, since the simplest thing of use may be just as well made pleasing and good in form and line, though that may be the only kind of beauty possible to it.

When we come to pottery the utility and adaptation to service influence is very obvious. Look at the form of a water-vessel, a pitcher we will say, as a typical form. It must have a large hollow body to hold as much water as can be conveniently carried by a single person, but not more than its handle or handles will lift. It must have a neck for pouring out. A rounded form is found to be more convenient for carrying than a square, and is easier to balance in the hand or on the head. The soft clay, too, readily takes the circular form on the wheel when the pitcher is formed under the hands of the potter; and the rounded form may be diminished towards the base, which saves weight, and at the same time gives opportunity for grace of line. Its form at once expresses its purpose of carrying and pouring. A nobler form is seen in the Greek hydria—a large three-handed water-vessel, adapted for carrying and pouring. It was carried on the head or the shoulders, the two side horizontal handles enabled it to be lifted up and down, while its vertical handle served the function of pouring.

We may note the similarity in contour and proportion of the Greek amphora or wine-vessel, to the lines of a woman's figure. It is, perhaps, the most graceful of the antique forms of vessels, and it seems dimly reflected even in the purely prosaic form of the modern bottle.

We might trace through all the various forms of vessels the clue of utility, and note how it determines their typical form as they are adapted, like the hydria or pitcher, for carrying and *pouring*: the amphora or ancient wine-bottle for keeping wine cool in the earth in portable quantities: the bucket type for *dipping* and carrying: the funnel type for *filling*.

The copper water-vessel of the Roman people seems to combine the functions of bucket and pitcher in a highly picturesque way, and its form enables a quantity to be carried on the head.

The *drinking* vessel again shows quite a different type of form, and in all its varieties declares its function—the cup, the glass, the tumbler, the mug, and the tankard.

In the bottle we approach again the type of the pitcher, the holding and pouring functions being again emphatic, throughout all its many shapes. The illustration shows a selection of the typical forms I have mentioned.

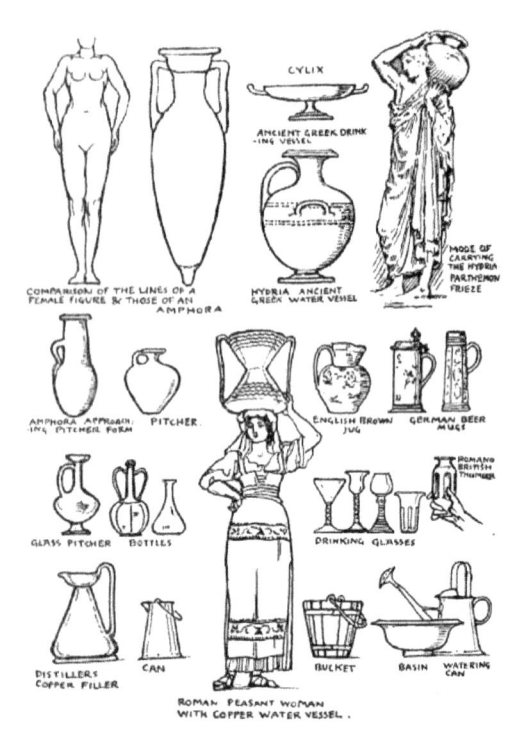

DRINKING VESSELS, ETC.

COMPARISON OF THE LINES OF A FEMALE FIGURE & THOSE OF AN AMPHORA.
CYLIX.
ANCIENT GREEK DRINKING VESSEL.
HYDRIA ANCIENT GREEK WATER VESSEL.
MODE OF CARRYING THE HYDRIA PARTHENON FRIEZE.
AMPHORA APPROACHING PITCHER FORM.
PITCHER.
ENGLISH BROWN JUG.
GERMAN BEER MUGS.
GLASS PITCHER.
BOTTLES.
DRINKING GLASSES.
ROMANO BRITISH THUMBER.
DISTILLERS COPPER FILLER.
CAN
ROMAN PEASANT WOMAN WITH COPPER WATER VESSEL.
BUCKET.
BASIN.
WATERING CAN.

The subject of the typical forms of vessels is very clearly illustrated in Meyer's "Handbook of Ornament," to which I may refer the student who wishes to pursue the subject further.

GERMAN BEER MUGS.

On the subject of bottles, however, I will just refer to a curious correspondence in design motive in two different materials.

ITALIAN FLASKS & BOTTLE.

The ordinary Italian oil or wine flask is one of the most charming of modern useful vessels. It is simply a piece of blown glass of the form first assumed by the molten glass when blown at the end of the glass-worker's tube. To make this primitive but elegant bottle portable and enable it to stand, it is bound around by a twist of rushes, or cane leaves twisted into a circular stand, and braced by vertical broader bands of the untwisted leaf at intervals, and a loop of the twist is twined around the neck, and left free to hang up or carry the vessel in. The whole is both highly practical and picturesque.

This is a type of Venetian glass bottle or decanter highly ornamented, in which the fundamental motive or idea of the protecting binding of rushes seems to be followed in glass. The melon-like divisions are defined by strings of raised glass laid on the surface, while the panels between are engraved in arabesques of leaves and birds, and the whole forms a very pretty piece of ornate glass design. (See illustration, p. 83.)

Here we have another instance of decorative motive derived from useful function, and of the adaptation in one material of a suggestion derived from another, though applied to the same type of form.

I have not mentioned the plate or dish type of vessel, which has on the whole, perhaps, received the most attention from the decorator of surfaces, perhaps on account of the more pictorial conditions its functional form presents.

There is a circular flat or concave surface in the centre of the dish, plate, or plaque to hold the food; and there is a circular space or rim for the hand, a border which will serve both as a frame to the central subject, and also to emphasize the edge. The Greek cylix, though really a shallow drinking cup, presents similar conditions to the designer, though more of the shallow boat or saucer type, and in the filling of these spaces the Greek vase-painter, as far as regards composition of line, dramatic action of figure, simplicity, and the necessary flatness and reserve, sets us the best models in this kind of design.

The Italian Renascence majolica and lustre ware give more sumptuous effect and more pictorial treatment, but are not nearly so safe a guide in taste as the Greek.

In pure ornament we cannot do better than study oriental models for the treatment of border and centre, and in the blue and white ware of China and Persia we shall find as satisfactory examples of decorative fitness as need be. The Chinese influence is freely and often very happily rendered in the blue and white ware of Delft, and in some of the works of the old English potteries, as Worcester and Derby for instance.

In textile design the functions of border, of field or filling, of wearing apparel, or furniture hangings and materials and their necessary adaptation to vertical or horizontal positions, differentiates the various types and classes of design in woven or printed stuffs. Here use again influences and decides decorative motive.

We recognize at once the essential differences of expression in different pattern plans and systems of line in horizontal extension, which mark them off as suitable for borders demanding linear, or meandering, or running patterns to fulfil their function of defining the edge, as in a garment or hanging, or in pottery, or forming a setting for the centre, as in a carpet.

PITCHER FROM ROTHENBURG. (SEE CHAP. III)

THE HANDLE OF THE PLATE.

PLATE & DISH DECORATION.

DELFT DISH.
CHINESE PLATE PATTERNS.

For these reasons, bearing in mind the constructive suggestion of their origin, the typical examples given of border systems have held their own from the earliest times as fundamentally adaptable to horizontal extension, while they also adapt themselves to endless variation in design and treatment.

Just as, for the same reasons, the systems of pattern adapted for indefinite extension over a surface (both vertically and horizontally), and represented by the plans I have termed persistent, have held, and still hold, their place in the world of design. These latter, too, it will be noticed, are all constructed upon, or controlled by, the same basis—the rectangular diaper.

There seems something fixed and fundamental about these linear constructive bases of pattern design from the point of view of what might be termed decorative or linear logic, and apart from their origin in actual constructive necessity before spoken of, and, as far as soundness of principle can guide us in designing, we cannot go wrong in obeying them, however various the superstructure of floral fancy we may build upon them. The acknowledgment of the principle alone, of course, will not make us successful designers, any more than the skeleton makes a living figure. We cannot do without thought, fancy, and vivifying imagination, guided by the sense of beauty, as well as of use, to produce design worth having in any direction.

To trace out this clue of utility fully and adequately through all the varieties of the vast province of artistic design would need, not a single chapter, but a large and amply illustrated volume. I have only attempted to call your attention to certain typical forms and instances where the bearings of the necessities of use and service have decided those forms, and must always influence the decorative designer, who should never forget them for a moment.

I. TYPICAL BORDER SYSTEMS.

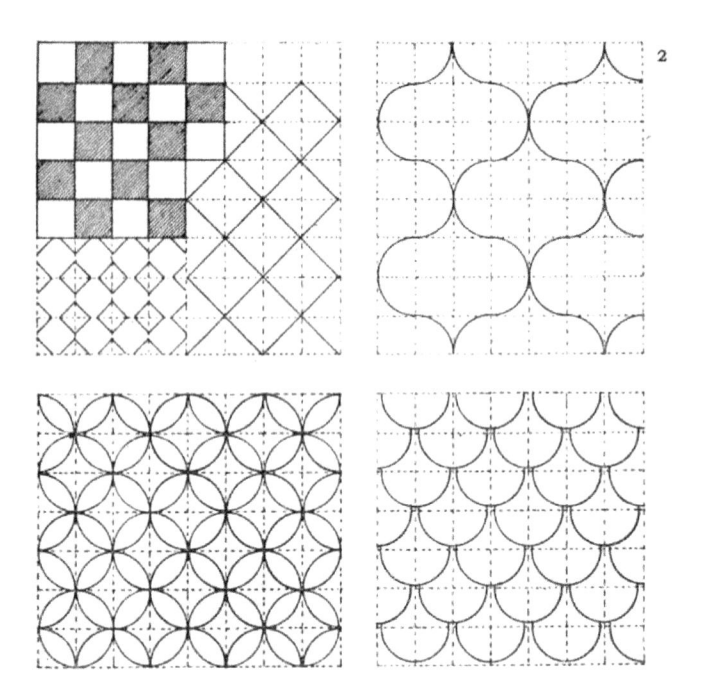

2. PERSISTENT PATTERN PLANS, RECTANGULAR BASIS.

Nothing has degraded the form of common things so much as a mistaken love of ornament. The production of things of beauty for ordinary use has declined with the gradual separation of artist and craftsman. Decoration, or ornament, we have been too much accustomed to consider as accidental and unrelated addition to an object, not as *an essential expression and organic part of it*; not as a *beauty which may satisfy us in simple line, form, or proportion, combined with fitness to purpose, even without any surface ornament at all*. The more we are able to keep before our minds the place and purpose of any design we have to make, the more we realize the conditions of use and service of which it must be a part, as well as the capacities of the material of which it is to be made; and the more we understand its constructive necessities, the more successful our design is likely to be, and the nearer we shall approach to bridging the unfortunate gulf which too often exists between the designer and the craftsman.

CHAPTER III.—OF THE INFLUENCE OF MATERIAL AND METHOD

WE have seen (1) that architectural considerations lie at the basis of design and control its general character, its scale, and relationships; and (2) that utility determines and specializes its particular forms and functions; now, as our third proposition, we may say that, in addition to these in limitation of material and methods of workmanship, we shall find the influences which determine primarily the purely artistic question of *treatment* in design, and which differentiate its classes and varieties.

If we look at a piece of stone-carving and compare it with a piece of wood-carving, for instance,—or, still better, take mallet and chisel in hand and experiment upon a piece of stone or marble, and try to evolve or to express a form by these means, and with a chisel, or knife, work upon wood—we shall soon find that the differences of the quality of the two substances upon which we work—the differences of density, toughness, resistance to the tool—at once demand different methods of handling each. Short, quick following strokes in the case of chiselling stone, and a longer, steady sort of pushing or driving movement, the chisel being held in both hands, in the case of wood-carving. From such necessary and fundamental differences the artist would soon develop a distinct style in the treatment of each kind of work. He would not attempt to make the stone look like wood, or persuade the wood to look like stone; but he would rather rejoice in their fundamental differences of quality, and make his work in each emphasize their essential and distinctive characteristics. These different characteristics are shown in the design and treatment of the carved stone corbel given, as compared with the misereres in wood; the stone-work being also controlled by the necessity of the jointing in the masonry.

CORBEL, 14th C^{ent}, DENNINGTON CHURCH, SUFFOLK.

WOOD CARVING. MISERERE, ST. DAVID'S CATHEDRAL.

In handling soft materials, like modelling clay, for instance, we encounter quite a different set of conditions. There is much less restriction of material and method, although the plasticity of the clay brings its own difficulties of manipulation with it. Modelling, indeed, it is soon perceived, is the reverse of carving, since in carving form is produced by cutting away, in modelling form is produced by building up (or adding to); surface being gained in the first case by delicate chiselling of sharp tools upon a close-grained, tough material, and in modelling by a delicate pressure of the fingers, or tools, upon a soft and sensitive clay.

Clay modelling, again, not being a final form, but rather a preparatory stage in design, bears to bronze, or plaster, much the same relationship as a design or drawing on paper for reproduction by a particular process bears to its finished form in the material for which it is intended. Clay has, it is true, after firing, a permanent form in terra-cotta, which of course thoroughly illustrates the freedom and naturalism of treatment of which it is capable; on the one hand associating itself with domestic use and adornment, kindred with the work of the painter, and on the other uniting itself with architecture, and being adaptable to all kinds of enrichment upon brick buildings.

WOOD CARVING. MISERERE, ST. DAVID'S CATHEDRAL.

SCANDINAVIAN CLAY VESSEL.

The adaptability and plasticity of clay, again, is shown in what might be called its fundamental capacity as thrown upon the potter's wheel. Here, under the steady revolution of the horizontal circular disk, or wheel, controlled and held in its place by the left hand of the potter, while he manipulates and varies the form with the right, we see how readily the clay obeys the law of the circular pressure and movement, and how, in obedience to it, every variety of form which the history of pottery displays becomes possible to it in the hands of a skilful and tasteful craftsman. Manual skill of a very accomplished kind is demanded in throwing, as anyone may see for himself by trying to form a vessel upon the wheel, simple as the operation looks, controlled by a purely mechanical movement. Then, in addition to dexterity in manipulating the clay and skill in forming the vessel truly, and of an even thickness, there is room for any amount of artistic judgment and taste in deciding the final form, or section, which the vessel shall take; and again, in the design and use of such ornament as shall express its form and office, or give it an additional decorative surface beauty.

With the use of ornament, indented while our clay is soft, or with raised moulding and edges, or low relief work, we are still carrying out the fundamental suggestiveness of the material and what may be called its natural method; and we find that ornamentation upon pottery in its earliest development took the form of indented zigzag borders and patterns, and to this day in some kinds of German pottery, and that known as Grès de Flandres, we find the patterns indented in outline and filled afterwards with the blue colour and glazed; the modern Egyptian red clay pots are ornamented with indented, cut, and raised patterns; while in the homely brown jug of our English potteries, we see the application of the principle of relief work in the quaint figures stamped upon the surface, pleasing enough, though without any reference to classic dignity or proportion.

There is a good instance of the pleasant use of stamping the pattern upon a clay vessel in this German pitcher from Rothenburg (see p. 87), bought from the workshop of the potter himself, who made the pots of the local clay, fired them, and glazed them himself, and finally was his own salesman—an instructive combination of functions not often found in our own country.

MODERN EGYPTIAN POTTERY.

With wax, modelling can be carried to a greater degree of fineness and sharpness of detail, especially upon a small scale. It is a material, therefore, which lends itself to modelling for bronze and other fine metal castings, to metals and coinage, as well as to small figures, lamps, various vessels and ornaments; and also to large scale, highly finished statues, especially when intended to be cast by the *cera perduta* or lost wax method, by which the molten metal from the furnace is made to flow into the mould, to take the place of the wax of the model, the wax of course melting and flowing out through the vents contrived for the purpose.

The figure is modelled in the usual way in clay first. Then a plaster piece-mould is taken, and into the inside of this, when taken off, the wax is pressed, so as to line it completely. A framework or skeleton of iron bars having been constructed to support the weight, the hollow mould inside the wax lining or skin, which represents the thickness of the bronze statue, is then filled up with a core composed of brick-dust and plaster, mixed in a paste and poured in. The ducts to enable the molten bronze to flow properly into the mould are then arranged, with vents for the escape of the melted wax and air. The plaster piece-mould is then carefully taken off, and the statue is disclosed in wax. This wax surface can then be finally finished by the modeller before the whole statue is covered in with another mould made of a fine paste of bone ash and Tripoli powder and other ingredients. It is then bedded in earth or sand, and the bronze, being mixed and melted in the furnace is run out into the ducts of the mould; when cool the mould is broken off, and, the bronze taking the place of the wax which is melted and escapes, the statue is complete.

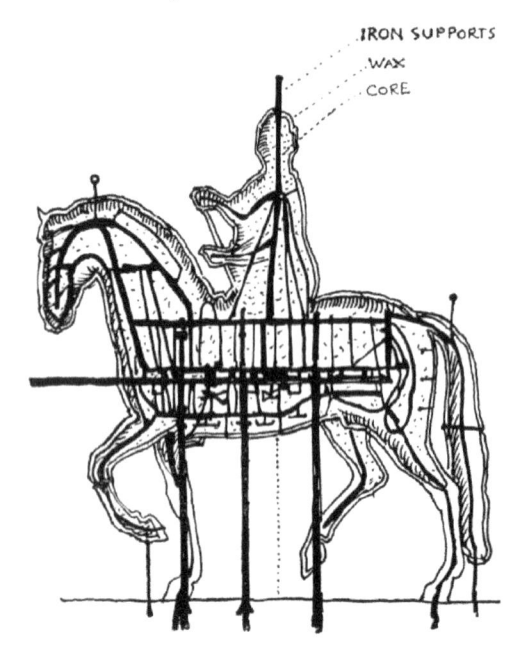

BRONZE STATUE OF LOUIS XV. BY BOUCHARDON, SHOWING INTERNAL IRON-WORK AND CORE.[3]

Thus a complete and perfect casting is obtained of the work, it being only necessary to stop the places where the ducts and vents were fixed, which by ingenuity could be arranged to occur in the less important parts. *Cera perduta*, as its name indicates, is an old Italian method, and was used by Benvenuto Cellini. It has been revived by Mr. George Simonds, who has given an account of it, and by our younger school of sculptors, Messrs. Alfred Gilbert, Onslow Ford, Harry Bates, and others, in place of the method of casting without the use of the wax, which entailed a great deal of surface work and chasing upon the hard bronze, so that the delicate modelled surface—the touch of the artist, in short—was lost, but it is just this which is preserved by the lost wax process, so that it is a method which favours artistic modelling, since it perpetuates it in bronze with greater precision than by the ordinary method, and does not require after touching in the hard.

In iron-work we have another strictly conditioned kind, in which design owes its character and peculiar beauty to the necessities and limitations of the material and mode of working. I am speaking of wrought iron, and of the forms in which it is usually found—in grills of all kinds, in gates, and railings. Now we may consider that the designer in iron has a material to deal with which is capable, under heat and the hammer, of obeying much invention and lines of grace and fancy. We start with a bar of iron; we plan our main framework; we may use rigid verticals and horizontals in forming our grill. A simple square trellis is the fundamental grill, but we seek more play and fancy. Our iron bar is capable of being twisted at its ends into spiral curves under heat, with the pincers (or even without, if thin). It is also capable of being beaten out with the hammer into flattened leaf forms, which again, by heating, can be worked and elaborated, and parts joined by welding in great variety of form. But we may consider primarily that the designer in iron starts with the bar, the spiral curve, and the flat leaf, or even only the first two. These are his units out of which he constructs his pattern; his pencils are the hammer and pincers, his easel is the vice, his medium is the forge. His business is to make a harmony in iron, and these are his notes, his treble and bass. His success will depend, firstly, upon the effectiveness with which he contrives to meet the fundamental purpose of the grill or gate, that it shall be a sensible and practical grill or gate to begin with; secondly, his lines and curves, however simple, must be harmoniously arranged, so that the eye is satisfied at the same time as the constructive sense; and thirdly, any invention or play of fancy which he can super-add without injuring the first two considerations will be so much to the good, and to his credit, and the common pleasure.

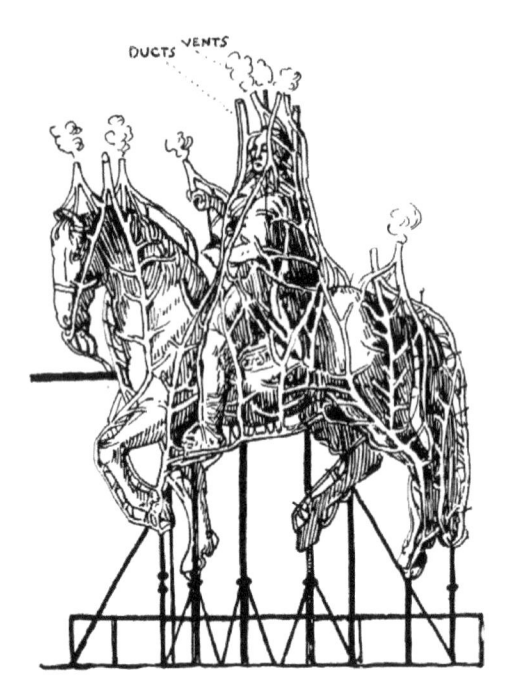

BRONZE STATUE OF LOUIS XV. BY BOUCHARDON, SHOWING DISTRIBUTION OF DUCTS AND VENTS.[4]

It is well, however, to test our powers by simple problems at first. If we cannot combine a great variety of attractive forms harmoniously, and fit them to useful purpose, let us try what we can do with few and simple forms. If we fail at constructing gates of Paradise let us see if we cannot make a good railing. If we cannot invent a romantic knocker, let us try our hands at an effective scraper. It is much better to do a simple thing well, than a complex or ambitious thing badly; and there is far more need in the world for well-designed and beautiful common things than for elaborate exceptional things.

WROUGHT-IRON GATES, ST. LAWRENCE, NUREMBERG.

THE IRON WORKERS UNITS.
WROUGHT IRON WORK PORCH GATES, CATHEDRAL OF S. LAWRENCE, NUREMBERG.

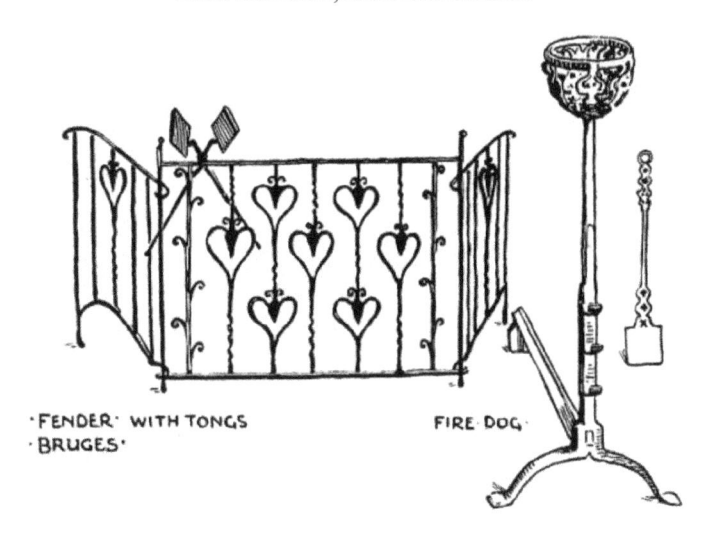

WROUGHT-IRON FENDER, TONGS, FIRE-DOG AND SHOVEL, BRUGES.

FENDER WITH TONGS BRUGES.
FIRE DOG.

WROUGHT-IRON ALTAR SCREEN, ST. THOMAS'S, SALISBURY.

PART OF ALTAR SCREEN IN WROUGHT IRON, CH. OF S THOMAS, SALISBURY.

A study of iron-work should be useful to all students in design, as showing what ornamental effects can be gained by economy of means, the effectiveness of simply repeating well-chosen curves, spirals, and lines; as well as the amount of fantasy and feeling which an inventive designer and craftsman can put into such work in its more complex and elaborate forms, and, above all, how perfectly it may be made to unite serviceableness and beauty; while, perhaps more conspicuously than most kinds of artistic work, it illustrates the essential unity of material and method with their results in design.

WROUGHT-IRON BALUSTRADE, ROTHENBURG, from a sketch by R. PHENÉ SPIERS.

The illustrations given exemplify different varieties of treatment, and also show how design in iron-work, in addition to the influence of the material, is controlled by the spirit and period of the architecture of which it becomes part.

We see this in comparing the free Gothic and rather fantastic forms of the gates of the south porch of S. Laurence at Nuremberg with the symmetric and formal screen from S. Thomas's, Salisbury (seventeenth or eighteenth century), or both with the flowing Renascence scroll balustrade from Rothenburg.

A most important branch of design is that of textiles, whether we regard it in its close association with daily life and the wants of humanity, with domestic comfort, personal adornment, or ecclesiastical splendour. It is, perhaps, the most intimate of the arts of design, and here again we shall find the control of material and method always asserting themselves.

Textile designing may be broadly divided into two main kinds: (1) that which is an incorporated part of the textile itself, as in woven patterns, carpets, and tapestry; and (2) that which is designed as a surface decoration to be printed or worked on the textile, as in cotton, cloth, cretonne, silk, velvet, and embroidery.

Into the many technicalities and complexities of the modern power-loom it is not now necessary to enter; but the main essential conditions it is always necessary for the textile designer to have in mind are that his design has to be produced by the crossing of threads in the loom, by warp and weft, as the sets of threads are called—the warp being the vertical threads, forming the web and foundation of the fabric; the woof or weft being the horizontal thread woven through it at right angles.

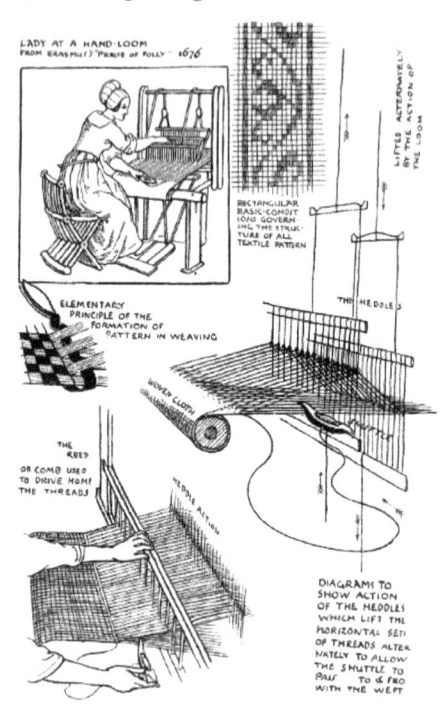

LADY AT A HAND LOOM, from Erasmus's "Praise of Folly" (1676).

DIAGRAMS SHOWING THE PRINCIPLES OF THE LOOM.

RECTANGULAR BASIC CONDITIONS GOVERNING THE STRUCTURE OF ALL TEXTILE PATTERN.
ELEMENTARY PRINCIPAL OF THE FORMATION OF PATTERN IN WEAVING.
THE REED OR COMB USED TO DRIVE HOME THE THREADS.
DIAGRAMS TO SHOW ACTION OF THE HEDDLES WHICH LIFT THE HORIZONTAL SETS OF THREADS ALTERNATELY TO ALLOW THE SHUTTLE TO PASS TO & FRO WITH THE WEFT.

In the simple low warp hand-loom, the warp being in two sets, the alternate threads are lifted by the heddles alternately. These heddles are connected with treadles worked by the feet of the weaver, who, with his hand, passes his shuttle with the woof backwards and forwards through the interstices thus left, and weaves the plain cloth. To make patterns, various wefts in different colours are added. This is the fundamental simple principle of weaving, which in a still simpler form may be seen in the making of tapestry and carpets in the high warp loom, where the threads of the warp are stretched vertically upon rollers in a framework, at which the worker sits and works in by his hands the different colours of the pattern horizontally, twisting and knotting the threads in through the warps on which the pattern has been marked, and pressing it together by a sort of comb to make it firm and solid; as the fabric is completed it is rolled up upon the roller.

Penelope is seen working at such a loom in a Greek vase painting. The simple hand-loom, as it was in the seventeenth century, is seen in the figure taken from Erasmus's "Praise of Folly."

What chiefly concerns the designer in woven textiles, therefore, is that he must be prepared for the necessity that his design must adapt itself to working out upon a square trellis of horizontal and vertical lines, which will represent his outlines, or the edges of his masses, in stepped outlines and edges, where the design crosses the warp diagonally at any angle, and in straight lines where it runs with the warp; since it may be said that pattern on woven cloth is produced by leaving out, or stopping out, certain threads in the wefts, disclosing one set in one place and another in another;   such threads corresponding with the holes cut in the cards placed in the loom to regulate the pattern, which are prepared from the design, after it has been worked out on squared paper to calculated intervals and numbers of threads or points to each line and mass of the pattern.

PERSIAN CARPET, SOUTH KENSINGTON MUSEUM.

Now, so far from wishing to conceal the characteristic flatness and squareness of outline and mass, which the nature of the conditions of weaving normally produce, the artist values these characteristics as essential to the work, and would make his design adaptable to them.

The most beautiful and decorative effects are produced in woven textiles by the contrast, harmony, and blending of coloured threads, wool, or silk, and the relief of one flat colour upon another, or one flat tint upon another shade of the same tint, so that anything like attempts at naturalistic drawing, and the representation of planes of light and shade and relief can only be clumsy, owing to the nature of the conditions, besides being mistaken, from the point of view of good pattern-work.

There are no better masters in the selection and treatment of natural forms in textile design than the Persians, who, in their magnificent carpets, show both the extreme of graceful conventional pattern, and also a happy mean in the treatment of flowers, trees, and animals, exhibiting in their drawing and colour definite characterization rather than naturalism; translating nature, as it were, and allying it with invention in a distinct region of their own. To do this is really what all designers should aim at, in whatsoever material they may work.

When we come to the second division of textile design, that in which pattern is applied to the surface of the cloth after it has been woven, by means of printing, the designer is chiefly controlled by considerations of scale and beauty of effect, as he has to adapt his design to various purposes, such as hangings and furniture coverings, or small dress patterns, kerchiefs, and so forth. Beyond the necessary limit of size of repeat and its satisfactory construction, he is freer than in designing for woven textiles; and, in fact, has about as much range as any other surface designer in colours.

It is considered a practical and economic advantage that a design should adapt itself to printing in many different schemes of colour, and be capable of treatment on a light or dark ground. In larger scale patterns, such as furniture cretonnes, patterns or parts of patterns are produced by a mordant or resist; that is to say, the light parts are printed in a mordant or chemical preparation which takes out the dye, and so discloses in those parts the natural colour of the cotton cloth. Similar effects can be produced by the reverse method of printing the cloth first with a resist and dyeing or printing the whole afterwards.

The methods and machinery of printing cotton have been carried to great perfection, and the necessary limitations as to what effects can or cannot be obtained are very few, what is done being largely regulated by considerations of cost. These apparent advantages, however, from the artistic point of view, expose us to new dangers. We may easily lose sight of the end in the very perfection of the means; the very facility of those means may lead the designer to forget that, after all, he is designing for a textile—something which will be hung in folds, variously draped, or worn. The desire to show the capacity of the method of printing a pattern in colours may not always be on all fours with the wish for tasteful design and reposeful effect. The fierce competition of trade, and the violent demands of the salesman, do not harmonize with the judgment of the artist. If you were in a company where all were talking at once at the top of their voices you would have to shout very loudly if you wanted to be heard, but no one would contend that these were the best conditions for the human voice. It is, however, a tolerably just simile of the present conditions of trade and their effect upon design. So long as things are made primarily to *sell*, rather than to last and live with, there will always be this difficulty and disparity between art and commerce; but a school of art can only concern itself with what are the best methods, and endeavour always to set up the best types of design, the best standards of taste.

If we want to represent flowers, for instance, in their natural superficial aspects of light and shade and relief, the natural form for such renderings is the still life study; the natural means, the canvas, palette, and brushes, or Whatman and water-colour; the natural equipment, power of graphic drawing and knowledge of pictorial effect. But, whatever value, pictorial interest, and charm such studies may have, as such, with the charm of treatment, with the freedom of handling open to the pictorial artist, and with the direct personal touch, the value, pictorial interest, and charm and beauty would be entirely lost if they were done by the yard, and spread over acres of cotton. The particular conditions which give value to the individual pictorial study become utterly lost when the attempt is made to produce a pattern on the same principles. It is neither good pattern nor good painting; and the very best machine-painting can only give a more or less coarse rendering of hand-painting, and it is therefore a mistaken application of it to try. It requires no special artistic feeling or training to recognize a bunch of roses or poppies thrown in exaggerated relief on a flat surface; but it does require both to appreciate a design made of the same flowers, composed and coloured harmoniously in an ingenious repeat, and drawn firmly and delicately with an understanding of the character and construction of the plants, yet treated with fancy and invention, and, at the same time, meeting perfectly the nature of the material and the method of manufacture. These qualities I should enumerate as the real necessities in designing for printed fabrics, whether it is cotton cloth printed from the pattern engraved on copper rollers, or furniture cretonne printed from flat blocks. In either case, in providing the design, firmness and sharpness of line would be good, and precision of touch in laying in the colour.

The embroiderer, again, is comparatively free as to range of choice in treatment of surface design, which will be necessarily governed by purpose, position, and nature of material and method employed. The bold design and large scale detail which would be suitable for bed hangings and curtains in crewel work, such as we find in the Queen Anne period, would be obviously out of place in small panels of delicate fine silk-work. A greater approach to the colours and surfaces of nature, too, in silk-work may be attempted, as in the plumage of birds and the petals of flowers, as we see in

Chinese and Japanese silk embroideries, though the decorative principle of shading one colour with other tints of the same should be followed when shading is used, keeping the colour pure and brilliant, and never using black or brown for shadows on colours.

EMBROIDERY.

NATURAL DIRECTION OF STITCHES IN WORKING LEAVES, STEMS, FLOWERS, & FRUIT.
SILK EMBROIDERY HEIGHTENED WITH SILVER THREAD ITALIAN 16TH CENTURY.
JAPANESE KIMONO PRINTED PATTERN HEIGHTENED WITH GOLD & SILK EMBROIDERY IN PARTS.
PERSIAN EMBROIDERY SILK ON LINEN BOKHARA.

A certain natural convention, we might say, belongs to the conditions of material and method in embroidery, and is inseparable from the art of the expression of form by stitches. Following the same principle of such acknowledgment of necessary limitations which we find hold good in other decorative arts, the essential stitch method of the embroiderer should be rather emphasized than concealed, although it does not follow that in preparing designs to be embroidered the stitches need be all represented, so long as the design is clear and plain, and the outlines distinct; while in the choice of the direction of the stitches, as well as in their form and character, must be found the particular means of expressing varieties of surface and characteristics of form. In making leaves, for instance, one would naturally make the stitches radiate from the centre towards the point, while the character of tree stems is well expressed by carrying the stitches crossways over others laid vertically first, as, in addition to the suggestion of lines of bark, the double row of stitches has the effect of suggesting the projection of a rounded stem. For filling in large masses, or for meandering types of patterns and scroll-work, or bold outline, chain-stitch is very useful, and has a compact, solid effect. It is much used in Indian embroideries. The introduction of gold thread, so much found in all oriental embroidery, enriches and heightens the effects of the colours very much, and on the unbleached linens and muslins, where the pattern is quite light, it has a charming effect. The Japanese make very effective use of gold thread embroidery, in some cases carrying the whole of the work out in gold upon a dark ground, or using it as a partial enrichment on printed textiles such as *kimonos* or robes; in other kinds, notably in dark, rich, full-coloured embroidered hangings, by introducing disks of gold thread, formed by stitching the thread down upon the ground in closely twisted spiral forms, which catch the light very effectively when hung upon the wall.

There is, indeed, in the embroiderer's art immense range of both treatment and subject. It may be light and delicate, and restricted to one or two colours, or vie in fulness, richness, and depth of colour and splendour of effect with tapestry itself. It may adorn a child's quilt, or decorate an altar; it may touch the hem of a garment, or inform the cover of a book; nothing seems to be above or below it; and throughout its manifold adaptations it offers an attractive field to the designer and the worker who is not afraid of patient but not unrewarding labour.

As further exemplifying the influence of material and method, I may just touch upon another art, in our days the most popular and far-reaching, perhaps, of all—the art of design in black and white for the book and the newspaper.

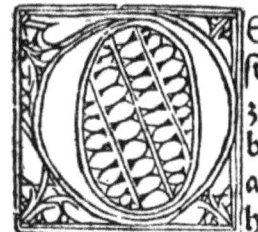

Er erste heymlich stheimbott oder stberg des teüfels sendt de menschē ze fahen dz ist die hochfart/der selb bott kumpt geritten/vnd sitzt auff ame Dromedari/vn ist mit guldim harnasch angelegt Vn fürt auff dē helm eīmē pfaben/ím dē schilt eīmen Adler In dem paner eīmē gekrönten Leo/vn ín dēr hand eīm braites schwert.

BUCH VON DEN SIEBEN TODSÜNDEN (AUGSBURG, 1474).

HANS BALDUNG GRÜN, "HORTULUS ANIMAE" (STRASSBURG, 1511).

Now, the early woodcut as we find it in the printed books of the fifteenth and sixteenth centuries owed its forms and qualities to the necessities of surface printing with types in a hand-press. The vigorous, bold drawing with the pen on the wood-block was cut by the engraver with a knife and on the *plank*, not as now, upon the cross section of the box tree: softer wood, too, was at first probably used. The engraver's knife left the artist's line firmer, perhaps, than it was drawn, and the design in vigorous open line was exactly adapted to print under the same pressure as the type had to undergo. The two were in true mechanical relation, and also in true artistic relation. The decorative effect of the early printers' pages is remarkably fine, and is obtained by very simple means.

With the decline of the severe and vigorous drawing of the great designers of the late Gothic and early Renascence period, and probably also with the invention of copper-plate engraving and printing, and the more rapid production of books, the art of the book printer declined, and the art of the book decorator with it; and although the woodcut still held its place, and was largely used for the next two centuries, and, indeed, down to our own time, in book ornaments, initial letters, and illustrations, it had fallen into inferior hands.

At the end of last century a sort of revival took place under Thomas Bewick and his school, which led, not to a revival of the firm and open linear drawing of the designers of the early printers, but rather to a search after extra fineness and qualities of tone and colour, hitherto associated with steel or copper-plate. This tendency or aim of the engravers, however, only served to put the woodcut out of relation with the type, and the type itself grew uglier, and was hardly considered as part of the artistic character of the book. William Blake seems to have been the only artist who made any attempt to consider the necessary relation of illustration and type, but he did it by means of copper-plate, and writing his own lettering.

It is only recently that a serious effort has been made to re-establish the old relationship between design and text in surface printing and as applied to books. Our newspapers and illustrated journals still print heavy black blocks, reproduced from wash drawings, along with thin pale type; and the tendency of the recent new photographic processes of reproducing the designs of artists has rather been to dislocate the decorative feeling and the relationship of type and picture aforesaid, by imposing no restrictions of material or method in preparing drawings for the press. We have now, however, a school of printers and designers in black and white who do consider decorative effect in printing and in the design of the printed page.

A CRADLE SONG

Sweet dreams form a shade,
O'er my lovely infants head.
Sweet dreams of pleasant streams,
By happy silent moony beams.

Sweet sleep with soft down.
Weave thy brows an infant crown.
Sweet sleep Angel mild,
Hover o'er my happy child.

Sweet smiles in the night,
Hover over my delight.
Sweet smiles Mothers smiles,
All the livelong night beguiles.

Sweet moans, dovelike sighs,
Chase not slumber from thy eyes,
Sweet moans, sweeter smiles,
All the dovelike moans beguiles.

Sleep sleep happy child,
All creation slept and smil'd.
Sleep sleep, happy sleep.
While o'er thee thy mother weep.

Sweet babe in thy face,
Holy image I can trace.
Sweet babe once like thee.
Thy maker lay and wept for me.
Wept

WILLIAM BLAKE.

Mr. William Morris, by his personal experiment and practice of printing, approaching it from the designer's point of view, has again placed the printing of books in the position of an art. By practical demonstration in the beautiful results of his work—in the beautiful books he issued from the Kelmscott Press—he has shown us what very fine decorative effects can be got by careful consideration of the form of the letters, by the placing of the type upon the page, by the use of good handmade paper, by the use of ornaments and initial letters of rich and bold design, harmonizing with the strength and richness of the type (which makes the ordinary types look pale and thin). His work, too, is obviously influencing printers and publishers generally, so that something like a renascence in printing and in design and decoration in black and white has been going on during the last few years.

Certainly a return to the practice of drawing in line is good, not only as a test of design and draughtsmanship, and absolutely necessary to all designers, but also as essential to designs or illustrations intended to contribute to the decorative character of the printed page.

In the various instances, therefore, to which I have drawn attention, we have seen that design in its many forms and applications must be reconciled to certain limitations of material and method; but that, so far from these limitations being a hindrance to harmonious expression or to beauty of result, they themselves, by their very nature, if properly understood and frankly acknowledged, lead to those very results of beauty and harmonious expression which come of that perfect unity of design, material, and method it is the object of all decorative art to attain.

CHAPTER IV.—ON THE INFLUENCE OF CONDITIONS IN DESIGN

IN the previous three chapters we have been considering Design under various conditions of use and material. The present may be considered as a continuation of the same line of thought in somewhat different directions.

We may consider conditions in the general sense as those general æsthetic laws governing the place and purpose of designs, and their position in relation to the eye and hand, such as height, plane of extension, and scale; or in the more particular sense which includes all these, as well as more strict technical conditions which, being accepted by the artistic faculty, influence the form and character of all design, the object being, of course, the attainment of the greatest beauty consistent with such conditions.

All design is necessarily conditioned, from the purely graphic and pictorial to the most abstract forms of decoration. We cannot set pencil to paper even without committing ourselves to a kind of compact with conditions. Here is a white expanse—a plain surface; here is something to make black marks with.

The artistic realization of or presentment of our thought, or our rendering of a piece of nature or of art will depend upon our frank acceptance of the natural limits of the capacity of pencil and paper—of plane, surface, line, and tint as conditions of representation, and on our faithfulness to them, by means of which we shall attain the most truth and beauty in drawing.

CEILING PAPER. DESIGNED BY WALTER CRANE.

CEILING PAPER. DESIGNED BY WALTER CRANE.

It is the recognition of this which gives distinction to all drawing, according to the individuality, invention, and character of the artist. We recognize his style and personality by his manner of dealing with the conditions of the work, and nowhere does this come out more emphatically than when those conditions are reduced to the simplest. So that in a line drawing in pen or pencil, in the economy of the means, and in the skill and mastery by which facts of nature, character, life, action, or beauty of line and ornamental effect are rendered by the simple use of outline, or tint, or solid black, we can recognise the artist of power just as clearly as we recognize a friend's handwriting.

CEILING PAPER. DESIGNED BY WALTER CRANE.

The suavity and grace of Raphael, the energy of Michael Angelo, the learning and finish of Leonardo, the sculptor-like definition of Mantegna, the firmness and care of Dürer, the breadth and richness of Holbein; all these qualities come out clearly enough in the studies and drawings of these masters in pen, pencil, and chalk. For beauty of style, treatment, and decorative feeling in pencil and chalk, perhaps few come near the studies of our modern master, Burne-Jones.

REPEATING PATTERN WALL-PAPER. DESIGNED BY WALTER CRANE.

In making studies, too, another condition comes in, important enough in its effects—that of *time*. In general practice no means to ends are more useful than rapid sketches and notes of passing actions and transient effects. In order to seize the essential facts quickly great economy of means is necessary, and practice and experience alone can teach us facility in selecting the leading points and most expressive lines. Given a limited time in which to note facts, the problem is how to set down the most truth in the simplest and most forcible way.

The conditions which govern the making of a sketch or study upon paper are sufficient as tests of artistic capacity, of draughtsmanship, of taste, and the other fine qualities which go to the making of a work of art, having what may be termed an independent or individual interest and value; but in adapting any kind of design to a definite ornamental purpose other conditions immediately come into play over and above those belonging to the conditions of draughtsmanship alone, conditions which at once influence the *style* of draughtsmanship and determine the treatment.

Again, everyone who attempts designs for different kinds of decorative purpose, for different materials, for different planes of extension, for different positions and uses, must perceive that such considerations are important factors in determining the plan, construction, and spirit of the design.

The ornamental conditions, for instance, which govern the design of wall-papers and hangings, demand patterns which climb upwards and spread laterally without any apparent effect or flaw in the repeat. Frieze designs, again, demand horizontal extension and definite rhythm, which latter is an important element in all border design.

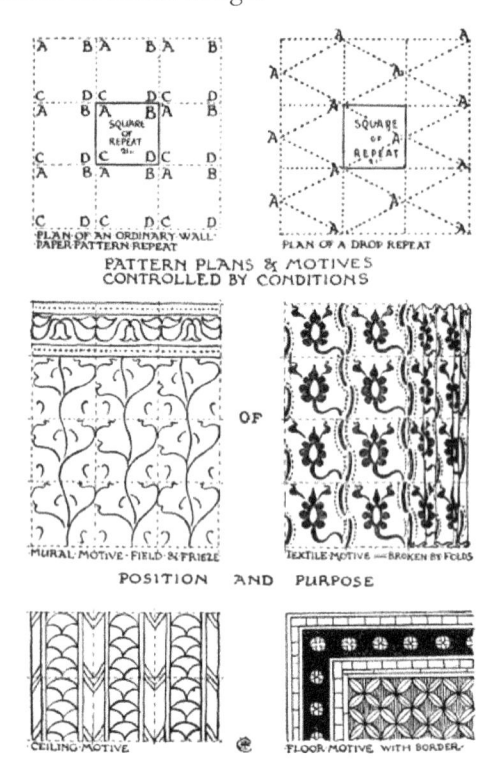

PATTERN PLANS & MOTIVES CONTROLLED BY CONDITIONS OF POSITION AND PURPOSE.

FLOOR MOTIVE. SKETCH DESIGN FOR INLAID WOOD, SOUTH LONDON FINE ART GALLERY. DESIGNED BY WALTER CRANE.

Designs for extension upon floors and pavements, where the effect of perspective distorts forms as they recede from the eye, require their own special planning and treatment, square, circular, diamond, and fish-scale plans being generally the safest, as bases, since they preserve their form in perspective better than irregular non-geometric or more complex plans.

Much the same kind of considerations control ceiling decoration, where, in addition, suggestions may be taken from constructive conditions, as, in flat ceilings, the design following parallel beams and joists and their interstices; the panelled arrangement of a coffered ceiling; or radiating spring of lines from constructive centres, as in vaulted ceilings.

Where a pattern will be broken by deep folds, as in textiles, in hangings, and curtains, the conditions favour the recurrence of bold masses, richer points, and more strongly defined forms, at intervals, than would be agreeable in a pattern for extension on a plane surface, unless we except carpets, where boldness of form and richness of colour are desirable.

Such conditions as these influence every department of decorative design, and in proportion to the completeness with which they are satisfied will depend the success of designs; and a design which may have less actual beauty, perhaps, than another, but which completely fulfils the conditions of its existence, is likely to have a longer life.

DROP REPEAT WALL-PAPER. DESIGNED BY WALTER CRANE.

The persistence of certain well-known types of pattern is probably due to this—such as the continual reappearance of the Greek fret in various forms as a border design in all sorts of work.

Questions of scale in design are less absolute, perhaps, since, though one may say as a rule that large types of design and detail belong to large rooms and large scale buildings, there may be interesting exceptions, when large patterns might suit even in a small room, if a particular artistic effect were sought.

The main condition in the matter of scale appears to be that we cannot afford to ignore the average human standard. As we may say that the human frame itself contains the elements and principles of all ornamental design, so its proportions and scale control the proportions and scale of all design. Objects intended for human use and service are bound to be of certain fixed or average sizes—seats and couches about eighteen inches from the ground, for instance; ordinary domestic doors not much over six feet high, and three feet six inches or four feet wide. The size of casements, again, is strictly related to the power of the hand to open them; while the sizes of all movable objects of use are in like manner strictly governed by the average size, height, and strength of mankind.

Pursuing the influence of such conditions, we find that there are in every direction natural limitations in every department of design: in the first place of scale and position in relation to eye and hand, in the second place of method and material.

Take the page of a printed book, for instance. The body of type impressed upon the paper, gives the proportions and dimensions of the page. The double page, when the book is opened to show the right and left hand pages (or recto and verso, as they are termed), is the true unit, not the single page.

DROP REPEAT WALL-PAPER. DESIGNED BY WALTER CRANE.

The type should be placed so as to leave the narrowest margin at the top and the inside, the broader on the outside, and the broadest of all at the foot. And this for obvious reasons, since in holding a book in our hand we naturally want the type brought well under the eye, the pages being set as close together as the necessities of joining down the middle will allow conveniently, so that the eye need not have to jump across a large brook of margin in travelling from one to the other, while the deep margin below enables the book to be held in the hand well set up before the eye, without touching the type.

In taking up a book with the intention of decorating or illustrating it, we must accept frankly these conditions, which indeed are, properly considered, a substantial help to the artist, just as the necessities of the ground plan give suggestions for the elevation in architectural design. These conditions, we may take it, are the architectural conditions of book-page construction.

The size, then, of our page-panel being fixed, as well as the page of type necessary to the book (sizes of books are, of course, determined by folding of the paper—folio, quarto, octavo, duodecimo, and so on), we are free to deal with it decoratively in a variety of ways, subject only to the acknowledgment of the essential condition that it *is* a book-page, and not a random sheet of paper to make blots of ink upon—or a stereoscope, or a card-basket, for instance, as some modern treatments of illustration in books suggest.

We may use the whole page for the design, surrounding it with a line or border. Or for the sake of richer and more ornate effect, while confining our picture or illustration to the limits of the type-page, we may use our margin for a decorative framework or border. As also in using ornamental initial letters the side borders can be utilized for ornaments branching up and down from the letter to emphasize the chapter or paragraph, in the manner of mediæval illuminated MSS., and in the way adopted by William Morris in his Kelmscott Press books.

Or, again, limiting our decoration to the actual type-page, we may divide the page at the opening of a chapter by a frieze-shaped panel or heading across the top, placing the initial letter below; or insert a picture in the text, occupying a half-page or quarter-page; or at the ending of a chapter design a tailpiece to fill the page where the type ends, treating any space within the limits of the type-page, which the type does not occupy, as a field for design, or placing one's pictures and ornaments in the midst or in place of the type.

The title-page, again, is capable of an immense variety of treatment, and great ornamental use can always be made of the lettering, whether accompanied by design or not.

I think, too, that it is obvious that the conditions of surface printing point to line-drawing as the most harmonious in effect for book illustration and decoration, as well as most practical mechanically, since type and blocks which decorate a page must be subjected to the same pressure. The form of letters, too, in movable type, being linear, whether Gothic or Roman letters, line-drawing is in direct decorative relation with the type.

OPEN FOLIO BOOK TO SHOW PROPORTIONS OF TYPE PAGE & MARGIN, KELMSCOTT PRESS, WILLIAM MORRIS.

TITLE PAGE FAERIE QUEENE WALTER CRANE.

W.C.

W.C

W.C

PAGE PLANS SHOWING VARIOUS ARRANGEMENTS OF TEXT & DECORATION

In proportion to the solidity or heaviness of the letters, too, as a general principle, stronger effects of black and white may be ventured on, while if the type is light and elegant, finer and more open-like work would be the most harmonious treatment. With the use of handmade paper, again, upon which a printed book always looks best, openness of line is a necessary condition in design work to be reproduced as surface printing blocks with the type, since the quality of the paper requires considerable pressure to bring up bright impressions, and under such pressure (with the grain and rough surface of the paper, which gives the richness to the lines and blocks of type or woodcut) fine and broken lines would print up too strong, and not look well. Pen or brush drawing, therefore, in firm and unbroken lines is the most adapted to the conditions in this case because they work and look the best, and lead to a distinct character and style.

Nothing looks worse, to my mind, than heavy toned and realistically treated wash drawings used with a thin and light type, such as we constantly see in newspapers and magazines.

The facility of the photographic processes for reproducing drawings of all kinds (as well as the decline of printing as an art before that, and the decline of good facsimile engraving), have no doubt tended to destroy the sense of style and harmony in combining text and illustration, since the two have come to be considered so entirely apart; but of late years there have been many indications of a return to sounder taste, which is sure to influence the printer's and illustrator's art more and more widely.

FROM "THE GLITTERING PLAIN," KELMSCOTT PRESS. DESIGNED BY WILLIAM MORRIS AND WALTER CRANE.

Chapter II. Evil tidings come to hand at Cleveland

NOT long had he worked ere he heard the sound of horse-hoofs once more, and he looked not up, but said to himself, "It is but the lads bringing back the teams from the acres, and riding fast and driving hard for joy of heart and in wantonness of youth" But the sound grew nearer and he looked up and saw over the turf wall of the garth the

FROM SPENSER'S "FAERIE QUEENE." DESIGNED BY WALTER CRANE.

O SACRED hunger of ambitious mindes,
And impotent desire of men to raine!
Whom neither dread of God, that devils bindes,
Nor lawes of men, that common-weales containe,
Nor bands of nature, that wilde beastes restraine,
Can keepe from outrage and from doing wrong,
Where they may hope a kingdome to obtaine:
No faithe so firme, no trust can be so strong,
No love so lasting then, that may enduren long.

Witness may Burbon be; whom all the bands
Which may a Knight assure had surely bound,
Untill the love of Lordship and of lands
Made him become most faithless and unsound:
And witness be Gerioneo found,
Who for like cause faire Belgè did oppresse,

And right and wrong most cruelly confound:
And so be now Grantorto, who no lesse
Then all the rest burst out to all outragiousnesse.

From books let us turn for further illustration to another source of illumination, namely, windows; where, in the design of leaded and stained glass, we shall find examples of another strictly conditioned and very beautiful province of design.

In the course of its historical development stained glass seems to show much the same or corresponding general characteristics at different periods as to style, as may be traced in other branches of art. The windows of the twelfth and thirteenth centuries were characterized by geometric pattern, and made up of small pieces of glass, the figure subjects small, set in geometric inclosures or quatrefoil panels and showing Byzantine influence in their treatment.[5] It may be, too, that the windows of the early Gothic period were influenced by the rich mosaic work of the Byzantine artists, but in the fourteenth and fifteenth centuries, as windows became larger and more important features in architecture, and stone tracery enabled very large openings to be filled with coloured and leaded glass, both the figures and the pieces of glass became larger, the general design more pictorial, till in the early sixteenth century we get perspectives and heavily-shaded figures, and large masses of light and dark, until the art perished in eighteenth century transparencies.

THIRTEENTH CENTURY GLASS FROM THE SAINTE CHAPELLE, PARIS (SOUTH KENSINGTON MUSEUM).

THIRTEENTH CENTURY GLASS FROM THE SAINTE CHAPELLE, PARIS (SOUTH KENSINGTON MUSEUM).

It perished because the essential fundamental conditions were ignored or not made important decorative use of. Leading, instead of being regarded as the backbone of the design, its fundamental anatomy, and essential decorative as well as mechanical characteristic, was rather looked upon as an awkward if necessary interruption in the picture, and the glass-painter, in endeavouring to follow the painter on canvas in his effects of relief and chiaroscuro, lost all the peculiar beauty and character of his own art without gaining the distinction of the one he would fain have rivalled.[6]

It has only been by artists going back to the fundamental conditions, and keeping faith with them, that a revival of glass-painting has taken place in our time.

Now we might divide design in glass into two parts:

1. Design in lead line.
2. Design in coloured light.

THIRTEENTH CENTURY GLASS FROM THE SAINTE CHAPELLE, PARIS (SOUTH KENSINGTON MUSEUM).

Both demand the full light of the sky to do them justice, but especially the colour work, and therefore can only effectively be used for windows placed high, or above the level of the eye, in the wall like church windows, for it is only the full strength of light which brings out the full beauty and depth which the best work in glass always possesses; and in some qualities of glass, indeed, only full sunlight will discover their inner heart of jewel-like colour.

Very beautiful effects in window glazing are produced by patterns formed of plain leads, and their value has of late been perceived by architects, who largely use them in domestic work. Either seen from within or without the effect is pleasant, and suggests a sense both of comfort and romance which refuse to be associated with large blank squares of plate glass and heavy sash windows, which require a Samson or a Sandow to lift.

Inside, the effect of large panes of plate glass is cold. Outside, it forms great holes in the architecture, but, with the use of leads, if the opening is large, there need be scarcely any diminution of light inside, while the network of lead forms a pleasant relief to the window surface and unites it by pattern with the architecture of the building.

The pliant grooved strip of lead, then, is the glass designer's outline. With it he weaves his plain pattern, which he can enrich with spots of colour or by jewels of light in escutcheons and roundels; and when he comes to planning an elaborate figure panel he is bound to contrive a well-constructed basis of leading to hold his colour and form together, and by means of its bold black bounding lines to define the masses of his pattern, each different tint of glass being inclosed by a lead line, and shading, faces, hands, and small details being added with brush drawing in brown upon the coloured glass.

SIXTEENTH CENTURY GLASS. FROM WINCHESTER COLLEGE CHAPEL (SOUTH KENSINGTON MUSEUM).

Apart from good design, well-planned leading and colour scheme, nearly everything depends upon the careful choice of tint in the glass itself, and immense pains and trouble are well spent in this way, since beauty of total effect, as well as particular harmonies, depend upon choice of the degree, depth, and quality of the coloured glass.

Now glass for colour work, called antique, is made in small sheets about 22 in. × 17 in. The sheets of one maker do not exceed 8 in. × 5 in. They may be classified as tints and whites. These form the palette of the stained glass artist, and furnish him with an immense range of tint and tone from which to select. But these, again, are divisible into two sorts: (1) what is called *pot-metal* self-colours, or sheets that are of the same metal throughout; and (2) that known as *flashed*, that is, when a thin skin of ruby, gold, pink, or blue is flashed upon a sheet of blue, white, pink, or amber. This flash may be lightened or removed at pleasure by fluoric acid.

The object of the maker of these small sheets of glass is to get as much variety as possible, not only in *light and dark*, which in the pot-metals is due to the varying thickness of the sheet, and in the flashed colours to the varying thickness of the flash, but in some cases a mixture of two or more colours in the same sheet, by which it will be seen that no two sheets even out of the same pot of metal are alike. It is the use of this variety and unexpectedness that are amongst the charms of stained glass.

We speak of *stained glass*, but in reality there is *only one stain*, properly speaking; other colours used on glass are enamels, the real colour being incorporated in the glass when made (pot-metal or flashed), and not painted on. This stain is a preparation of silver, and is mixed with a vegetable colour, yellow lake, to weaken it. It is principally used upon the whites to stain diapers, hair, etc., and when fixed in the kiln the yellow lake is burnt away, leaving a slight residue which is easily removed, and the silver is vitrified into the glass, the depth of yellow being varied according to the strength of the stain and the susceptibility of the glass.

In setting to work to design a stained glass window, it is usual first to make a coloured design to scale—1½ inch to the foot is the best.

A window may be composed of one light or of many, each separate panel inclosed by the masonry or mullions being termed *a light*. The question of treatment of subject as a single design extending across several lights, or as separate panels, must depend first upon the particular subject, or subjects, to be treated, then the scale of the window, and the general character of the architectural setting.

Supposing it is a subject like the Nativity, with the Adoration of the Magi, it would lend itself to treatment as a single subject extending across several lights, and to great richness and splendour of colour. The colour design in such a case would be the most important, but, as I have before said, it must be perfectly combined with, and built upon, a well-designed network of lead lines, those lines forming themselves essential elements in the design, defining the forms in bold outline, and uniting and giving value to the masses of colour. For while we may separate the problem into two parts, the design of lead lines and colour design, the window must be conceived as a whole, not merely as composition in line to be tinted.

Having made our scale sketch, the next step is to work out the full-sized cartoons, which, of course, demand more attention to drawing and detail. Many artists make as many elaborate studies for figures, drapery, and details as they would for a highly-wrought picture in oil, or mural painting. As a matter of fact, however, though any amount of good drawing and invention may be put into glass design, it should not be forgotten that beauty of pattern and effect and symbolic suggestion are the objects and not pictorial naturalism.

For main definition in the design the essential lead line is all important. It would not do to sketch in a figure in a casual way, and then surmount it with lead lines; it should be carefully considered as a piece of bold and massive outline design.

In leading we may use a bolder line for bounding and defining the main masses, and a thinner sort for subsidiary fittings; in this much will depend upon the scale of the work. The lead, which has a double groove, may be said to serve several functions. Its primary office is to hold the pieces of glass together: it forms the linework of the design, surrounding the figures and forms, separating them from each other and the background, as well as defining the secondary forms, as of drapery and other detail. Then, too, the lead joints ease the cutting of awkward shapes in the glass, which however should be avoided in planning the cartoon. Again, it may be used to obtain greater variety into large masses, as a piece of drapery, for instance.

THIRTEENTH CENTURY GLASS GRISAILLE, SALISBURY CATHEDRAL.

CARTOON FOR GLASS, SHOWING LEAD DESIGN, BY FORD MADOX BROWN.

CARTOON FOR GLASS, SHOWING LEAD DESIGN, BY FORD MADOX BROWN.

The cartoon being made, the next thing is to make the working drawing. This is done by laying a semi-transparent piece of paper over the cartoon, and tracing *merely* the lead lines and thus obtaining the skeleton of the window.

The glass is cut from this drawing, the cutter cutting the glass just within the lines, thus allowing for the heart of lead. The same drawing serves also for the leadworker to glaze the finished work upon.

The shapes of the whites and light colours are seen when the sheets are laid on the drawing; but the shapes of the dark colours, through which it is impossible to see the lead lines, must be obtained in another way.

The best way is to cut the shape in thin sheet glass, which is then placed on the dark sheet of antique glass held up to the light, and moved about until the most suitable part of the sheet is found. They are then laid on the bench together, and the piece of sheet glass is pounced with a small bag of fine whitening, which, when removed, leaves its shape on the dark sheet to be followed by the cutter's diamond.

We now come to the all-important task of selecting the glass.

The ordinary trade way of doing this is to number the outline, which indicates to the cutter certain racks correspondingly numbered containing the different colours. But if it is to be really careful artistic work the designer ought himself to select each piece for his work.

The principle and idea of colour in glass design, dealing as the artist does with pure translucent colour, is necessarily distinct from those obtaining in other kinds of painting, such as mural, when opaque colours and a variety of half-tones are used. The glass designer does not attempt to shade his figures and draperies by the light and dark parts of a sheet of coloured glass. He desires to express the jewel-like quality—the quintessence of colour in every piece of glass—by the force of contrast, not in the juxtaposition of dark and light pieces of one colour merely, but by the bold arrangement of various colours, having the effect of one, but with a richness and sonorousness that the single tint does not possess.

For example, in a yellow drapery we should take a rich decided yellow as keynote. Obviously if the adjoining pieces were of the same colour, the effect would be flat and tame; but if we take a low toned yellow or neutral colour, the keynote will be screwed up to concert pitch, as it were, and if the neutral colour is followed by a reddish tone of yellow and that by another variation of yellow, that again by a decided green, and so on, we shall achieve that desideratum in stained glass—*variety in unity*.

The general effect will be warmer or colder as reddish or greenish tones predominate in the scheme. Care, of course, must be taken to bring these contrasted—even discordant—component parts into a harmonious whole: indeed every piece should be selected, not only to agree with and help its neighbour, but with reference to the harmony of the whole. Any undue abruptness of contrast may be brought into sufficient relation by the after painting.

The white must be treated in the same way, a mixture of warm and cold tints as a rule, the general effect of each mass being made warmer or colder as found necessary. Great care must be taken with the masses of white to prevent them looking like holes in the window: for instance, a white coming next to a dark colour would have to be a tint (or very low in tone, as we should say in painting) to hold its proper place. Only by actual experience, however, can the artist learn how one colour affects another, and how certain combinations will look in their place.

We have now reached the painting stage. All the glass has been cut and laid out on the outline. It is now looked over to see if there are any pieces that will not stand the fire—that is, that would change colour or lose brilliance. The gold pinks, brown rubies, and some sorts of pure ruby are liable to do this. Pieces of plain sheet glass may therefore be cut to the same shape to paint on, to be afterwards glazed behind the coloured pieces, so that the full brilliance is preserved.

The wings of the angel in the panel by Mr. J. S. Sparrow (to whom I am indebted for this detailed account) have been treated in this way.

The outline was made in colours ground in turpentine, fattened and made workable with japanner's gold-size, in order to stand the matte of water-colour to be added afterwards.

MODERN GLASS, DESIGNED AND EXECUTED BY J. S. SPARROW.

When the figure is drawn in this way all the pieces are stuck upon an easel glass (a large stout piece of sheet) with a composition of bees-wax and resin. As this is the first time all the pieces have been seen together the panel is carefully looked over, as a whole, to see that each piece is of a right colour and value. Some pieces may have to be cut over again; others strengthened or modified *by the addition of another piece of glass.* This last method is called plating, by which rich and beautiful deep toned effects can be produced.

A strong flat matte of water-colour is now laid all over the figure. This forms the half-tones, and the lights are taken out (when dry) with hog-hair brushes, the colour being first loosened by modelling the broad lights with the finger, which indeed is the best implement, and as much of the modelling should be done by it as possible.

A quill may be used to take out sharp lights. The work should now be ready for the kiln, but before firing it should be again stuck up, and looked over, and any strengthening or definition added in shadows on details by oil-colour with the addition of fat turpentine to keep it open; the dry surface of the glass being first treated with a wash of oil of tar to make the colour flow easily.

Then the diapers and hair are stained on the back of the glass, and it is ready for the kiln.

After being leaded up, the leads soldered together at the junctions, the panel is again placed on the easel, and further alterations or improvements may be made, as the leaded panel looks very different from the glass by itself. The panel is next cemented, the leads filled up with putty or cement to make it firm and water-tight. The cement is like a very thick paint, a mixture of white lead, whitening, red lead, lamp-black, dryers and raw and boiled oil.

The window may require to be supported by horizontal iron bars, if it extends over two feet. They are usually placed about fifteen inches apart, as the leaded glass might bend under the pressure of wind without extra support.

From this account we may realize what care and taste are necessary to carry out really artistic work in stained glass. The whole subject affords us a good illustration of one of the highest and most beautiful of the arts of design, severely controlled by well-defined conditions—conditions which, if followed faithfully, give it all its peculiar character, strength, and beauty. The necessities of leading and cutting the glass demand a certain severity and simplicity of design—from which a new beauty is evolved, capable in its turn of influencing other forms of art for good, as in easel painting—which harmonizes with its symbolic and religious intention as well as with the architectural and monumental character of its surroundings in its noblest forms in public and college halls and churches; while its glow and colour, suggestive symbolism, or heraldic adornment, may cheer and vivify domestic interiors with a touch of poetry and romance.

CHAPTER V.—OF THE CLIMATIC INFLUENCE IN DESIGN—CHIEFLY IN REGARD TO COLOUR AND PATTERN

WE have seen how largely Design in its manifold forms has been influenced by various physical conditions and necessities, and in pursuing the subject we can hardly fail to note that, outside those more strictly defined technical conditions we have been considering, there are certain broad controlling influences which have determined, and still determine, essential differences of character as between the products of one country and another; differences which, despite the complex network of international commerce and exchange, tending ever to obscure and confuse those native and natural differences by mixture and fusion, still persist. Indeed, as Manchester manufacturers and merchants well know, in the matter of pattern and colour they have to be taken into serious account, since we have unfortunately taken upon ourselves the responsibility of supplying Eastern markets, substituting our own ideas of pattern and colour in fabrics for the original native ones—or rather, sending back to the native Chinese and Indian second-hand notions of their own colours and patterns.

Now to what principal cause may we trace these broad differences in the choice and treatment of colour and design in different countries—those variations which enable us to assign each to its native home, north, south, east, or west, upon this parti-coloured globe of ours?

If we were to endeavour to mark upon a chart in some bright colour, say red or yellow, all those countries where, given a certain organized social life of civilization of some kind, bright sunshine was the rule, and indicate proportionally its lesser degrees in others, we should get a vivid notion of the general distribution of the colour sense: we should naturally come to the conclusion that it is to the source of all our life, light, and heat—to the sun—that we must also trace our colour sense, which is a part of the sense of sight itself. It is to the influence of sunlight, direct or indirect, and to its prevalence in a greater or lesser degree in different countries, then, that we may attribute the differences of taste and feeling for colour and pattern which mark the different quarters of the inhabited earth.

We know how we are affected by the absence or presence of sunlight in our own country, and by a heavy or light atmosphere, and are sensitive to the changes of the weather, which no doubt have their influence upon our work, and we know how different colours look in different degrees and qualities of light.

We have only to follow the pattern book of Nature herself, indeed, and see how distinctly she paints upon the globe the different zones of climate in different coloured flowers, birds, and animals corresponding with those differences; or follow her system of coloration in the ordinary procession of the seasons, without going out of our own country.

With the return of the sun and lengthening days and the new awakening of life in the spring, a delicate bloom overspreads the landscape, the dark wintry woodlands burst into blossoms and clouds of foliage, taking every tint, from the palest green to delicate amber and red; while the meadows show the rich moist green of new springing grass, embroidered with flowers, yellow, white, and blue; and the blue sky seems to repeat itself in the copses where the hyacinths grow. Gradually, as spring turns to summer, the colours deepen, the greens of trees and grass grow fuller, the flowers grow brighter and more varied in hue, crimsons and reds and purples are seen, and gardens become feasts of colour; and as the cornfields ripen scarlet poppies mingle with the gold, and the leaves of the trees, having reached their darkest tint, as autumn nears, become tinged with yellow and brown, and, before they fall, turn into wonderful harmonies of russet and gold, in part recalling, though in lower tones, some of the colours of spring.

The ripe fruit in the orchards gives a deeper note of richer and brighter colour, when the procession of flowers has reached the threshold of winter, bare and cold, though not colourless—its colours being more metallic—the silver of frost and mists, and the ruddy gold of the winter sun gilding the black trees, whereon mosses and lichens take the place of leaves and flowers, and sombre yews and hollies and firs, instead of the bright greens of spring, until the whole is veiled in ice and snow.

This drama of expressive colour is enacted before our eyes every year—those of us, at least, who are fortunate enough to live in the country, and are observers; and even to town dwellers the tale of colour to a certain extent is told by the importation of flowers, or even by the textiles in drapers' windows, or costumes in the street, as humanity responds to the approach of the sun by wearing lighter and fairer colours in the spring and summer, and getting darker and more sombre again in the autumn and winter.

We have only to glance at the various manifestations of our home arts to note these changes with the characteristic colours of our varied landscape reflected, not only in the works of our painters, but in the half-tones of our textiles and wall-papers, and throughout our decorative design, which for form, too, owes so much to the flora of our native land.

It does not seem to follow that with the greatest amount of sunlight we get the *most* colour; on the contrary, the zenith of light is the absorption of colour, just as darkness represents its extinction. Light and darkness are the black and white on the palette of nature, necessary to give value to her colours.

The sense of colour, too, is no doubt greatly affected by other climatic influences, such as humidity, haziness, clearness, heat and cold, as well as their accompaniments in varieties of scenery and locality, such as plains or mountains, woodland, sea-board, lake, river, agricultural land, or wild nature.

We associate brilliant colours and bold designs with eastern and southern countries, but, apart from the greater stimulus of light which might encourage the use of vivid colour, there is, I think, another reason which accounts for the bolder and franker use of colour and ornament in the south and east. Broad and full sunlight has a curiously flattening effect upon colour and pattern, and therefore colours and patterns which under a gray sky would look staring, or very strong and striking, under the full sunlight fall into plane, and become subordinated to the dominant pitch of light.

We may take as an instance the porch of the Cathedral at Pistoia. The bold black and white bands of marble which face the front of this building—as of so many mediæval Lombardic Italian cathedrals, as at Florence, Genoa, and Siena (an idea borrowed from the Saracens)—look striking enough under a gray sky, but when the sunlight falls upon the building and raises the whole pitch of light the whole mass with its projections falls into planes of broad light and shade. The black bands become gray and flat in the light, and all fall into their places in the architectural scheme, and therefore, though borrowed from the east, are quite appropriate in a climate like Italy, which can count on persistent sunshine for the most part, summer and winter. Inside the porch, in the spandril and vault, is faced with Della Robbia ware, in blue, white, and yellow, and a very beautiful piece of decoration it is. This, again, however, in a dull atmosphere might look cold and strange, but illuminated by the rich reflected light cast up from the sunlit pavement it takes all sorts of accidental lights and falls into its place admirably. Otherwise the porch is interesting from the curious blend of Byzantine, Saracenic, and classical motives and influences in decoration.

PORCH of CATHEDRAL OF S. JACOPO PISTOIA

Seen in the cold and dull light of an English museum, away from their proper architectural surroundings, panels of Della Robbia ware are apt to look somewhat strong, bold, or rank in colour, which only shows they were designed in a sunny bright climate, and to be seen in a full external or warm reflected light as a rule. The very qualities that make the ware trying in one place make it right in another.

The various historic types of design in architecture and decoration are, in fact, mostly the result of the blending or uniting of elements derived from different sources. While we may in the leading types prevalent in different countries detect the fundamental prevailing influence of life, custom and habit, the result of climatic and racial conditions; we may also see, owing to social and political changes and the results of conquest or of commercial relations, other elements coming in various details of construction, form, and colour.

Our present purpose, however, is rather to seek the fundamental characteristic types and predilections traceable to the fundamental or natural conditions of locality and climate, as far as they can be followed in historic decoration.

It seems to have been in the power of certain ancient peoples to impress and to preserve the character of their life and the conditions of their habitat very strongly upon their art, so that, though their political power has long ago been swept away, their records remain practically imperishable in their monuments of art.

Of such the ancient Egyptians must always be typical.

If we look at the structure of the primitive Egyptian dwelling we shall find that it illustrates those influences of climate and locality in a very emphatic way.

In the first place, as we know, Egypt depends upon her great river, the Nile, which may be said to have made her existence possible, since its waters fertilize the whole country. It is interesting, then, to note that the primitive Egyptian dwelling was essentially suggestive of the riverside and of a country of sunshine. Its materials were those of the waterside, consisting of clay and canes and lotus reeds; the canes being used for the framing and support of the clay walls, which are built in layers between them.

The plans and diagrams of construction (from Viollet le Duc) will give a clear idea of the form and character of the primitive Egyptian dwelling. In the course of an interesting account of its construction he says: that it is a dwelling for a country where *brilliant sunshine is the rule* is shown by the smallness of the windows, which are furnished with lattices. The walls were frequently plastered with clay, covered with a composition made of the same clay and fine sand or white stone dust, and this furnished a ground for the painters who decorated the reeds and plastered walls with brilliant colours; the walls and ceilings of the interior were also decorated in the same way; rush mats furnished the floor and covered the lower part of the walls. Sometimes, also, we find a portico supported on bundles of reeds, the covering of which is made of wood and byblos, with a terrace of clay before the door, affording shade and coolness in front of the dwelling. Like most dwellings in eastern countries, there is a flat roof or terrace on the top of the house, approached by steps; and here awnings are spread on poles to give shade, when they can be used for sitting upon or for sleeping or enjoying the cool of the day.

Primitive Egyptian House, after Viollet le Duc

COLUMN FROM TEMPLE OF LUXOR.

When the Egyptians learned the art of building and carving in stone from the rock dwellers above the Delta, and built their great temples, they still perpetuated in stone, in the reeded and filleted columns with lotus capitals, the ornamental traditions of the reed-built primitive dwelling, and the painter still adorned them in bright primitive colours; so that we are perpetually reminded of the great riverside, from which sprung the flower of that ancient art and civilization. Another effect of climate upon art may be noted in the representation of figures. The Egyptian climate being extremely warm but equable, most out-door occupations precluded the wearing of much apparel, so that the figure nude and lightly clad plays an important part in Egyptian design, as in Greek.

At a time like the present, when the world of design suffers rather from what might be called too generous or too mixed a diet; when the tendency is to over-elaborate, to combine too many elements; to be lost either in an overdone flamboyance of curvature, or in a straining after a forced and inappropriate naturalism, a study of Egyptian art may be recommended as a wholesome corrective. The simplicity, severity, and restraint, abstract and yet vivid characterization of form, frank and primitive coloration, purposeful intention, and mural motives and methods are full of suggestiveness and value to the student and decorative designer.

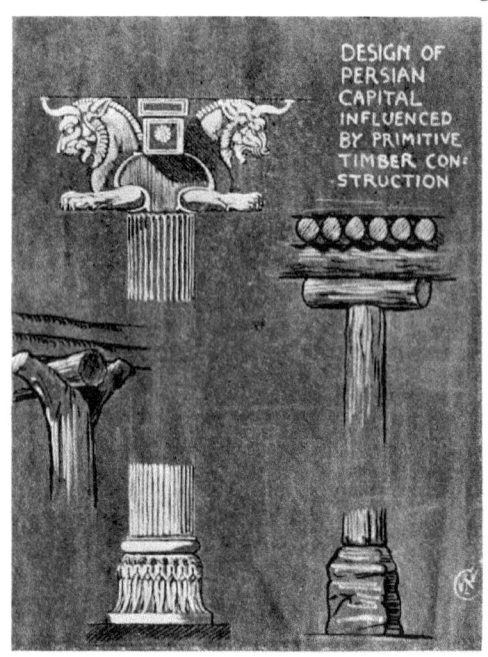

DESIGN OF PERSIAN CAPITAL INFLUENCED BY PRIMITIVE TIMBER CONSTRUCTION

LOTUS CAPITAL, PHILÆ.

Another instance of the influence of primitive timber construction over stone may be seen in comparing the ancient Persian column with its timber prototype still in use. Persia, indeed, is another eastern country which has preserved almost unbroken traditions in design from a very remote past, and may be said to be the source of the most beautiful types of ornamental art the world has ever seen, and especially in three leading forms—coloured and glazed tiles and bricks, pottery, and textiles. To judge from the wonderful decoration of glazed bricks discovered a few years ago at Susa, forming part of the ancient forum and palace of Darius, destroyed in the reign of Xerxes, B.C. 485-465, excavated by M. and Mme. Dieulafoy,[7] the artistic skill of the Persians in this kind of work, and their sense of its value, and the treatment of colour and ornament, dates back to a very early period.

In the famous frieze of archers, which formed part of the wall decoration of this palace, the figures are frankly repeated in design though alternating in the patterns and colours of their dress, boldly relieved upon a field of turquoise blue, formed by the glazed bricks by which the frieze is constructed. The figures and ornament must have been moulded or stamped in relief upon the clay while soft, and cut up into bricks, and afterwards fired and glazed in the method of Robbia ware; the whole scheme is severely simple but very effective in its proper position upon the walls of one of the large courts of the palace, mostly in reflected light under projecting porticoes, and would be very impressive and at the same time truly mural and reposeful in feeling and colour.

Such a scheme of frank colour and fine detail could hardly have been conceived except in a country of brilliant light. Some doubt exists as to the exact position of the frieze upon the wall. Figures of similar scale in Assyrian work and also at Persepolis were placed not far, if at all, above the eye level.

Upon the dress of one set of the archers is figured, it is supposed, the fortress of Susa itself, which was built upon a mount.

There is much interesting ornamental detail in the dresses, which afford excellent authorities for the costume of Persian warriors of that period. We see also the palm-leaf border, a primitive form, type and forerunner of a whole tribe of border design. The rosette is said to resemble "the full-blown Star of Bethlehem, conspicuous among all other flowers, among the herbage clothing the stretches of Susiana and the tablelands of Iran (Persia) after the first rains in early spring." (Perrot and Chipiez, p. 137.)

We may note, too, what seems obviously the prototype of the Moorish battlement, defined in blue bricks above the figures, suggesting they are guarding the citadel.

FRIEZE IN COLOURED AND GLAZED BRICKS, PALACE OF SUSA. FROM THE REPRODUCTION AT SOUTH KENSINGTON.

The Moorish or Arabian form constantly occurs as an ornamental cresting in carved woodwork, and also appears to have suggested an ornamental form largely used with variations in eastern carpets, notably those of Turkistan.

The treatment of the design has the severity and simplicity of early Asiatic monumental art, and is allied in treatment to the Assyrian relief work, but is more subtle and refined, and shows a finer decorative and colour sense.

In the treatment of blue the Persians always seem to have been particularly successful, and their later tile work in the Mohammedan period is well known, and continues down to our own time.

The love of blue and its use in tile work and pottery seems to have been general all over the east; it may be because of the adaptability of the metallic oxide colour to firing, but also it may be due to the pleasant relief and sense of coolness such decoration would afford to the eye in courts and interiors screened from the sun.

The old Nankin blue, so famous in Chinese porcelain, in the so-called hawthorn pattern, was described by one of the emperors as the blue of the sky showing through the white clouds after the south rain.

In carpets Persia about our sixteenth century reached a pitch of perfection in design, colouring, and material which, it would seem, has never been reached before or since. In these works we, of course, pass to a very different and much later period of Persian history, after the Arabian invasion in the seventh century, and the conversion of its people to the Mohammedan religion, under which Persian art developed in such delicate, rich, and beautiful forms.

There are very magnificent specimens of the finest types of Persian carpets now in the national collection at South Kensington, the Persian collection having been recently rearranged in the new galleries in Imperial Institute Road to very great advantage as regards lighting and opportunities of study.

The famous Holy Carpet of the mosque at Ardebil is perhaps the finest example, though there are others more inventive in pattern, if not more delicate in design or harmonious in colour. A curious feature in the pattern of this carpet is a hanging lamp, such a lamp as is used for lighting mosques, with a painted glass body, probably suspended by chains from the roof. The lamp is repeated at the end of the main ornament of the field of the carpet, facing opposite ways.

The inscription worked in Arabic characters into the carpet at one end is given in translation thus: "I have no refuge in the world other than thy threshold. My head has no protection other than this porchway, the work of the slave of this holy place, Maksond of Kashan in the year 946" (corresponding to our A.D. 1540). We thus see that it is a carpet destined for an entrance, or *porchway*, of a mosque, and the woven images of the lamps probably indicated the real lamps suspended overhead to light the entrance to the mosque. So that, though they seem strange objects in the pattern of a carpet, they have a certain appropriateness and significance in this particular one. Fire, too, was a sacred emblem of the ancient Persians.

Persia might be said to be a country of gardens, of deserts, and of abundant sunshine. It is for the most part a high table-land, and is described as a climate of extremes. "Nowhere in the habitable world is there so sharp a contrast between the heat of noon and the cold of night, between the brown bare rock and the verdant meadow, between the gorgeous hues of natural plains and the absolute bareness of arid wastes." (Perrot and Chipiez.)

Such a description is very suggestive. We seem to see natural reasons for the interest and beauty of Persian art in the varied physical conditions of their country and climate.

The love of the sheltered, walled-in, and natural garden is very evident in their literature; and the influence of their flora upon their design of all kinds is evident enough.

The idea of the eastern paradise is a garden. We have it in the Bible in the Garden of Eden—an inclosed pleasance or park full of choice trees and rare flowers, animals of the chase, and birds. This idea recurs constantly in Persian design. The very scheme of the typical carpet seems derived from it—a rich vari-coloured field hedged about with its borders. The field is frequently obviously intended for a field of flowers, and sometimes suggests a wood or an orchard of fruit trees. The idea of the green oasis to the traveller in the desert; the grateful relief of the colour and shade of green trees and fresh flowers; the sound of waters; the delight of the horseman and the hunter; the dark forest full of dangerous animals—are not these things irresistibly suggested in Persian design?

HOLY CARPET OF THE MOSQUE AT ARDEBIL (SOUTH KENSINGTON MUSEUM).

The same sensitiveness to natural beauty and the influence of climate is shown in their poets. The astronomer-poet of Persia, Omar Khayyám, sings of the awakening spring. It is a period, too, associated with the termination of a religious fast, Ramazan, which is analogous to our Lent, perhaps.

Omar invites his reader to come forth, like a true poet, seeking inspiration in the wilderness.

"With me along the strip of herbage strown,
That just divides the desert from the sown,
Where name of slave and sultan is forgot,
And peace to Mahmud on his golden throne."

Spring in Persia must be a much more sudden burst of life and efflorescence than we can realize from our own timid and coy climate. Even in Italy the spring generally comes all at once with a burst of bloom and a profusion of blossoms and flowers, and in its strength the sun straightway leads on into summer before one is aware. This gives one an idea what it must be in a country like Persia—the country of the rose and the nightingale as well as of the vine, of which Omar the poet is eloquent.

Then, too, it is an agricultural country. "He who guides a plough does a pious deed" is one of the precepts of the early Parsee religion, which also, as its main conception, presents the constant strife of good against evil, light against darkness, personified by the contest of Ormuzd and Ahriman.

The sturdy and honest peasant was the backbone of the country in ancient times, and furnished those sturdy warriors who built the power of the ancient kings. And in the political changes or conquests to which Persia has been subject in the course of her history, her people would always appear to have had a recuperative power, or a power of absorbing their conquerors, or perhaps a certain tenacity of purpose, or a conservation of the vital part in old beliefs and traditions which have been favourable to art.

How far that art was original, in the time of Persia's ancient greatness as a conquering power, in the time of Darius, when the palace at Susa was built—how far it was influenced from other sources, or contributed to by artists of other nations, must always be more or less a matter of conjecture; but in the Susa work we are reminded of Assyrian decoration, and even of Greek and Egyptian influence.

The Persian art, however, which has had the most influence upon the neighbouring Asiatic countries, and upon Europe, has been produced since the Arabian conquest in the seventh century, and the conversion of the country to the Mohammedan faith. Even then, however, although in Mohammedan art the representation of animals is forbidden, the Persians were neutral and independent; in Persian design animals have been freely introduced, and with charming decorative effect. It is supposed, indeed, that Persian art is really the source of invention of many forms commonly called Arabian and Indian, and these forms have travelled both east and west, and have been modified in the countries of their adoption. The Persians seem to have been in Asia much what the Greeks were in Europe—both great adaptors and great originators in design.

One might trace elements and influences and types of form and treatment from other countries and races in Persian art, but one traces Persian influence to a far greater extent in the art of other countries.

In India, which was also invaded by Islam, and was colonized by Persians, the Arabic type of art also became naturalized in architecture and decoration. Here again we have a country of the sun. Here again we find tile decoration in great beauty, and the use of bright colours and intricate design. Intricacy both of colour and pattern is perhaps the chief characteristic of Indian design.

One feature in Indian, as in Arabic dwellings, may be noticed as a direct result of the persistent sunshine turned to decorative account—one common to eastern countries—the pierced screen or lattice window, which tempers the fierce light of the sun and breaks it into small stars of light.

The rich carved timber overhanging windows, with its lattice screen so characteristic of old Cairo and Arabian life, is repeated with variations in India, and not only in wood but in stone and faïence. We find small ogee-pointed windows with perforated lattices cut in sandstone of intricate design and delightful ornamental effect. There are some in the India Museum from Agra. But the loveliest of all are those in the mosque of the Palace at Ahmedabad, consisting of most delicate and intricate designs of trees cut in stone, which fill the arched openings. One of these windows is here illustrated. There is nothing more delicate or beautiful in the whole range of architectural ornament.

ARAB CASEMENT FROM CAIRO (SOUTH KENSINGTON MUSEUM. DRAWN BY W. CLEOBURY).

In the tomb of Yusuf Shah Cadez, at Multan, occur large perforated screens in tile work. This tomb, an excellent reproduction of which is to be seen in the India Museum, is a fine example of Mohammedan tile work and decoration in two blues—turquoise and ultramarine—on a warm white ground. In the luminous atmosphere of India, beneath the deep blue vault of the sky, such colour on such surface must be very beautiful.

Perhaps the love of intricate ornament in Indian carved and pierced work in the doors, window casements, and lattices may be due in part to the certainty of obtaining a bright, crisp, rich, sparkling effect in the broad and strong sunlight, where every touch would tell, and the fret or lattice work over a pierced opening would have all the richness and delicacy of lace.

Then in the solemn and dimly-lighted splendour of the interior of the mosques, the Mohammedan, alike in Arabia, Turkey, Persia, or India, found a grateful contrast and relief to the eye, while his religious imagination and emotion were stimulated. Much the same feeling intensified which comes over one who passes from the brilliant Venetian sunlight on the piazza, the glittering quays and dancing light and colour of Venice, into the subdued, cool, and golden shade of St. Mark's.

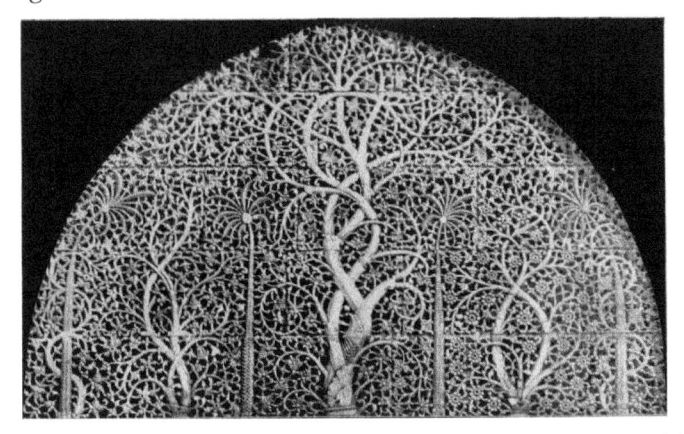

INDIA. CARVED STONE LATTICE WINDOW FROM THE MOSQUE OF THE PALACE OF AHMEDABAD.

This wonderful contrast of bright and dark, of glitter and solemnity, the splendour of sunlight and the solemnity of shade, can only be fully appreciated in southern or eastern countries. The pitch of light being higher the shade seems deeper, and yet it is a shade full of colour always. When the sun sinks, in the short afterglow everything seems fused in an atmosphere of luminous colour and half-tone, which transfigures and glorifies everything. We get an approach to it on the finest summer evenings in England, but with a different and generally less romantic background. It would appear, though, that climates which are characterized by constant sunlight and heat favour rather traditional than individual forms of art. The sun, the giver of life and light, becomes overpowering, always present, and in its searching beams leaves no hiding-place for the romantic imagination, except in temples and mosques at sunrise or sunset, or under the moon. We may have an equable and warm climate like Egypt, where all is sharply defined in the light of a clear and serene atmosphere, with a regulated, ordered life, as in her ancient days, under a long succession of dynasties, and we see the outcome in art—measured, calculated according to strict method and authority and convention, with but little room for individual feeling.

In Persia we find a climate of sharp contrasts, hot sun by day and sharp cold at night, verdure and desert, bare rock and flowery meadow side by side, and we get a wonderfully varied art, rich in colour and fantasy.

In India the invention, though kindred, perhaps even largely borrowed, seems tamer, the intricacy more calculated, the richness more mechanical; and we find this with a dependent people in a land of fiercer and more permanent sunshine, pursuing mostly an agricultural life, like the ancient Egyptians, under conditions practically unchanged for centuries.

In Greece, which fused and absorbed Asiatic elements in her art, we see another country of the sun, yet subject to winds and variations and marked transition of the seasons—a mountainous, rocky country, beautiful in form and embracing the sea. In art she has given us the perfection of figure sculpture.

In Italy, with hardly less sun, yet by no means beyond the reach of wintry cold, severe winds, great rains and sometimes snow, yet with a burning summer for the most part, which has decidedly fixed the types in her architecture, we find a union of many elements, a halfway house between east and west, where Asiatic feeling unites with Greek and Roman, Saracen and Norman, Gothic with Renascence, in an unexampled wealth and profusion of inventive design in architecture, sculpture, painting, and all the family of artistic handicrafts, which makes her a happy hunting ground for the artist, an inexhaustible treasure-house of beauty and suggestion.

We might follow the chariot of the sun, from the land of its rising, Japan, a climate more near to our own, and note her wonderful display of manipulation and imitative skill, in all ways of handicrafts dominating by a certain grotesqueness as well as naturalistic impressionism; or, passing to her great foe China, see something of the same tendencies and stages in the rising of her art, breaking off, as it were, at a stage of restrained conventionalism—or westward, along the southern shores of the blue Mediterranean, following in the footsteps of the Moors, and note the wonderfully ornate but somewhat heartless splendour of their art in Spain: the gilded magnificence of the Alhambra, with its glittering pendentive ceilings, borrowed, as some think, in the first place from Persia, and the wonderful jewel-like sparkle and intricate fancy of its ornament with its ever-recurring star-forms and scimitar-like scrolls.

And then turning northwards into France, with one hand touching the sunny south and the other dipped in the gray English Channel, we should find some of the same elements, but very differently mixed, with a very distinct character of art. Cold in colour, correct in form, brilliant in workmanship, quick-witted, dramatic; ever experimenting and inquiring, and desiring, like the ancient Greeks, some new thing.

Pursuing our journey northwards, we might pause in Flanders and Holland and mark how closely associated with local conditions of life and climate are their forms of art, more especially as illustrated in the art of their past days—the pictures of rich Flemish burgher life of the Middle Ages, the knights and ladies with a certain sternness and stiffness of demeanour, as of an energetic and yet patient people accustomed to contend with difficulties, proud, yet devotional, and fond of comfort, kneeling, well-clad in velvets and rich furs against a northern climate.

SPAIN. PORTION OF THE ALHAMBRA. DRAWN BY GUSTAVE DORÉ.

Germany would tell a similar tale in her arts, though with a more dominant military and religious note, more fantasy and more melancholy, and with a wild grotesque element corresponding with her more varied conditions of climate and scenery. The latter quality is still more marked among the old towns of Bohemia. The two sketches here give some of the architectural characteristics of both town and country dwellings.

OLD HOUSE IN TURNOV, BOHEMIA, DATED 1816.

STREET IN EGER, BOHEMIA.

After such a journey we should doubtless be glad to get home again to our own varying and changeable climate, and when seated comfortably at the fireside think how much the characteristics of our native art may also owe to the influence of the constant and varied procession of sunshine and cloud, storm and calm, heat and cold, fickle spring, short summer, long uncertain winter, our mist and rain (which gives us our green woodlands and meadows), to our wild and dangerous coasts. Or we may well think whether these influences are not traceable in our art: love of domesticity and indoor comfort, characterized by warm and blended though subdued colour, small patterns, trimness and neatness; love of animals and flowers, of natural scenery and the sea. May it not be said these are characteristics which our pictorial art certainly displays? While our architecture (in spite of foreign importations) is obliged to consider the necessities of a varying climate, so that our houses are built as a rule more to live in than to look at; and the colours of our interiors, while they often re-echo the greens, browns, and russets of our landscape—as our patterns and fabrics recall the flower gardens and meadows—are chosen perhaps more to live with quietly than to excite controversy, or compel a reference to the grammar of ornament.

CHAPTER VI.—OF THE RACIAL INFLUENCE IN DESIGN

THOSE personal predilections and idiosyncrasies which we each possess, those differences of temper and qualities of perception which affect our sense of colour and form, which account for those variations of treatment in the rendering, in design or drawing, of the same objects by different persons—what are these and whence do they come? They belong to the very constitution of our minds and bodies; they are beyond our own control, and beyond almost our own consciousness, oftentimes. They belong to our progenitors and ancestors perhaps as much as to ourselves, and are lost in the broken records of past family histories; we can only say that certain forms and colours appear so and so to our eyes, that we delight in some more than others—because we are made that way. Such indications of character and preferences are generally traceable, where clues and records exist, to *the race*, or mixture of races from which we have sprung. We attribute, for instance, certain imaginative faculties to our Celtic origin; certain calculating and analytical capacities to Teutonic sources; while as a mixed race we call ourselves Anglo-Saxon, and as such are supposed to be especially distinguished by practicality, the racial type gradually, in the process of time, being formed by the collective action of such small individual characteristics—somewhat as great geological deposits, such as our chalk hills, have been formed by the gradual accumulation and aggregation of the minute shells of minuter marine creatures.

These typical racial characteristics in art—these preferences in colour, form, pattern, treatment, sentiment, and idea, have left their marks upon the history of art, which indeed becomes, finally, the *only* history of races—the only record left of peoples to tell us of their intimate life, their hopes and fears, their struggles and their aspirations, so that a scrap of wall-painting, a fragment of an incised slab, a piece of broken pottery, a weapon of bronze, or a jewel, become in course of time full of significance—eloquent books of the life of peoples and powers long ago covered by the drifting sands of time.

The desire to record and to perpetuate seems to have stimulated the primitive artistic instinct in all races; and, indeed, it may still be said to be a living factor and motive in art production.

Each race seeks an image of itself (as every individual desires a portrait), and strives to put in imperishable form the character of its own life, and the ideas or ideals dearest to it. Thus, the prehistoric hunter left images of the animals he hunted, and his hunting reminiscences, scratched upon bones and smooth slates and stones; much as the Assyrian kings, in a more elaborate way, having the resources of a powerful civilization at command, loved to have recorded on sculptured slabs, lining their palaces, their prowess in arms and the chase; more especially as hunters and slayers of lions, though in their case the lion hunting was done in a more luxurious modern way, the animals being driven into special inclosures, and let loose on purpose to be slain by the king and his men—a system of a piece with the generally tyrannical and cruel methods of despotic persons. Still, no doubt, there was considerably more risk and danger involved than in a modern battue in a pheasant cover—barring the chance of being shot by your neighbour's gun.

Certainly the general tenor of the story told in ancient Asiatic art is that of the conqueror's triumphs, of the strong overcoming the weak, the glorification of kings and warriors in battle, of beleaguered cities, and the carrying away of captives and spoils. No doubt, if this conquering spirit had been absent, if each branch of the great human family had remained within its primitive borders, their art would have presented sharper and more distinct contrasts, while remaining simple in character. It is the restless, exploring, conquering, acquisitive spirit which mixes and blends elements originally distinct—well, it may be it also acts as the stormy wind that scatters the winged seeds of design and, bearing them to new soils, produces new varieties.

It is difficult, of course, to disentangle the strictly racial characteristics in art entirely from those other strong influences which, in fact, may be said to have helped in their formation—the influence of climate, habit, and local materials, which we have previously touched upon. Yet the purely human element appears to come in, and the final form which art takes among a people must bear the stamp of individual choice as well as of collective sentiment and climatic influence.

In primitive communities, however, the individual is less apparent than the collective racial influence. The forms of art are typical and symbolical rather than imitative or graphic. The great Asiatic races of antiquity, to judge from the remains of their monuments, the palaces of their kings, and their temples and tombs, adopted certain typical methods of representation which, in the case of the ancient Egyptians, became, in association with a strictly ordered and carefully organized social existence under an elaborate religious system and ritual, actual forms of language and record in the hieroglyphic. These consisted of certain abstract representations of familiar forms and figures inclosed in a kind of cartouche, incised upon stone walls, or stamped upon plaster and filled with colour.

The lotus flower served as a symbol of the annual overflow of the Nile (at the summer solstice) so important to the Egyptians; the ram and the sun symbolized Amru-Ra, the king of all gods; other animals, with and without wings, the cat, the dog, the sparrow-hawk for the soul, the beetle (*scarabæus*) for creative energy, generation and perpetuation of life, the snake for continuity of time, etc.; and even differently arranged lines, the zigzag for water, the circle, square, waved line, spiral, labyrinth, etc., betokened the divine and secretly-working powers of nature.

EGYPTIAN HIEROGLYPHICS. TOMB OF BENI HASAN. NINETEENTH DYNASTY.

Such forms inclosed in cartouches massed together, sometimes in horizontal lines, sometimes in vertical, formed a striking wall decoration in themselves. A wonderful pitch of abstract yet exact characterization of natural form was reached by very simple means in this picture-writing. The birds especially are remarkable for their truth. Every object had to be clearly defined so as to be recognized at once and easily deciphered. The profile view of an object is always the most characteristic and typical, and lends itself best to a system of representation where all objects are on the same plane. So the glyphic artist kept strictly to profile.

Love of typical form, definite outline and mass, flat and vivid coloration—these are always characteristic of ancient Egyptian art, even when, as during the eighteenth and nineteenth dynasties, a freer style and greater naturalism is apparent in their portrait sculpture and wall-paintings.

ALTAR WITH OFFERINGS. EGYPTIAN MURAL PAINTING, THEBES.

The love of clearness of statement and their conception of art, as in the nature of a decorative record, seems to be emphatically expressed in their ways of representation. For instance, in painting an altar piled with offerings they give the altar front in elevation, but the offerings, in order that each and all should be seen drawn in profile, are arranged in ground plan. Thus we may say that their statements were pictures, their pictures were statements.

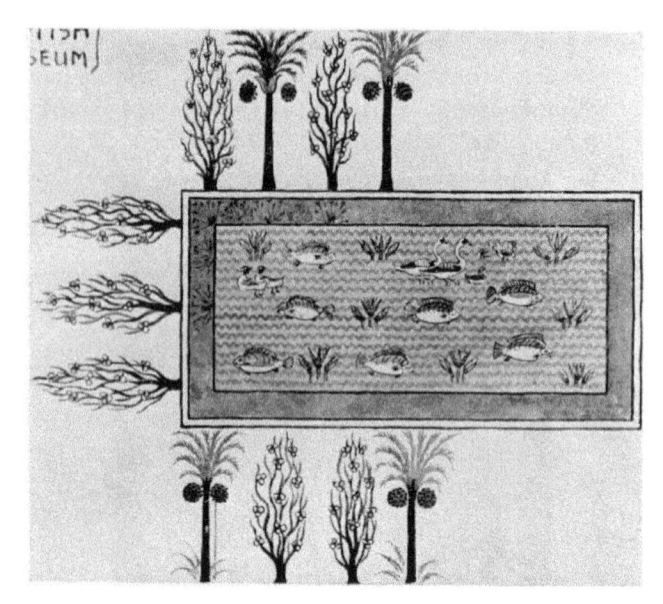

EGYPTIAN WALL-PAINTING (BRITISH MUSEUM).

ASSYRIAN TREE OF LIFE.

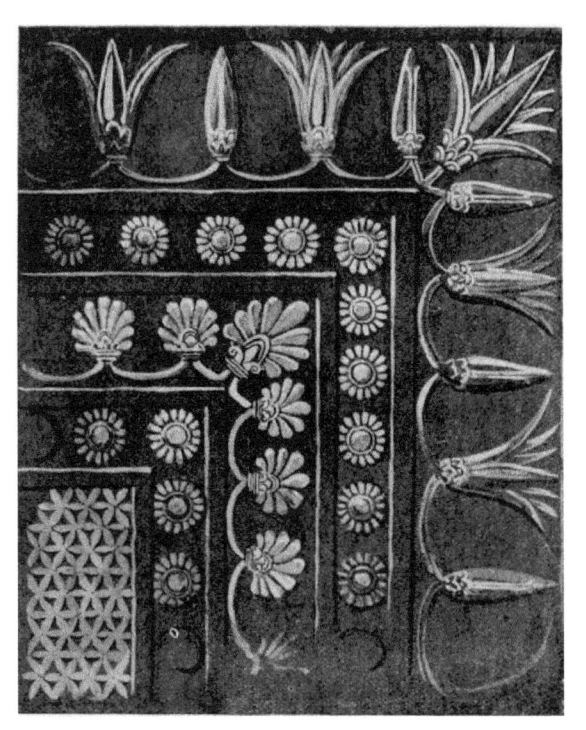

ASSYRIAN BAS-RELIEF. PAVEMENT SLAB (BRITISH MUSEUM).

There is a wall-painting in the British Museum showing a fish pond or tank in a garden, surrounded by trees. The inclosed water is rendered by a flat tint of pale blue, with horizontal zigzag lines in a second tint across it. Lotus flowers and buds spring vertically from it, and on its surface ducks and fish are painted in profile. The trees are painted on the upper side and ends with their stems springing from the edge of the pond; but the row of trees on the near side grows with the tops towards the water; while the row at each end sprouts outward. The whole forms a very pretty piece of ornament, and would embroider well for a table-cloth centre, or lend itself to a treatment for a mosaic floor. Note the way in which the trees alternate (apple trees and date palms), and the grouping of the ducks and the fish alternating with the lotus flower. It is freely painted with direct brush touches on the white plaster.

ASSYRIAN TREATMENT OF NATURAL FORM SLAB 76 BRIT. MUS.

In the ornamental treatment of tree forms all the eastern races seem to have excelled. Trees have always been associated with religious belief, and have had mystical and symbolical significance—as the tree of the garden of Genesis, the tree of life, and the fatal tree of the knowledge of good and evil. Trees, too, were man's first shelter and dwelling; no wonder a race descended from arboreal ancestors should revere them and hold them sacred.

VINE & FIG TREES FROM ASSYRIAN SLABS BRITISH MUSEUM N.25.

It is interesting to compare this Egyptian rendering of the date palm tree with an Assyrian rendering of the same tree, though the latter is sculptured; or, again, with the Græco-Roman version at the house of Icarius. The typical and sacred tree with the Assyrians, however, was the tree of life, which became with them a formal piece of ornament. In it we seem to see, too, the original form of a type of ornament constantly recurring in the art of all the Asiatic races, and which was apparently carried by them, or from them, into Europe; reappearing in Persian, Greek, Roman, and Renascence work in all manner of variations, remaining a typical horizontal border motive to our own day.

The lotus appears in sculptured Assyrian pavements on the outer border, the open flowers alternating with the buds, as in Egyptian work. Then we have another typical and constantly recurring border motive in the rosette, which has a rich and sumptuous effect, closely filled in this way. Then comes in the palmette, or tree of life, while the centre filling, a network formed of a six-petalled flower form, again recalls the suggested textile origin of the ornamental motive of the whole, to which I have before alluded.

Other interesting and characteristic renderings of flowers and trees may be found in bas-relief upon the Assyrian alabaster slabs used as wall decorations, such as those showing the vine, the fig, the lily, and the daisy here given, the sculpture of which, in general, is remarkable not only for the combination of great power of expression and energy of action with a very dominant formalizing and ornamental and typical treatment of form, but also for great delicacy of chiselling; in one slab there is a small figure of a king in his chariot, inclosed within larger work, as finely cut almost as a gem or seal. Note, as illustrating the ornamental treatment of animal forms, so characteristic of these Assyrian or Semitic sculptures, the way the lions are carved, the masses of the hair of the manes carefully marked and ornamentally designed, the muscular lines of the face emphasized in the same ornamental manner. The result is a typical lion, stately, monumental, sculptural, and decorative, yet in no way wanting in energy of action, character, and vigour.

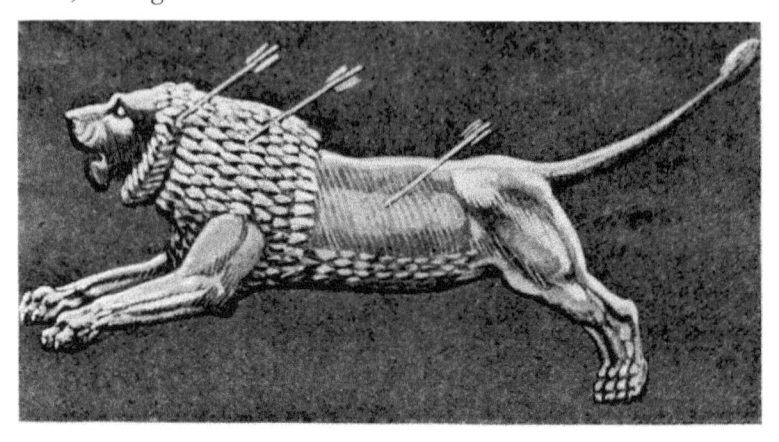

ASSUR BENI PAL. ASSYRIAN LION FROM BRITISH MUSEUM.

ASSUR BENI PAL. ASSYRIAN LION FROM BRITISH MUSEUM.

Nothing could be more different in spirit and style from the ordinary modern European sculptor's treatment. The Assyrian grasped the essential leonine character, but expressed it in typical and ornamental terms. The modern English, French, German, or Italian generally seeks a naturalism which struggles to escape from the conditions of the material; he seeks accidents rather than essentials, and, in his horror of formalism, tries to treat the masses of hair and mane as if he wielded the painter's brush rather than the sculptor's chisel—though it is generally modelled in clay first before it is carved. The result is loss of dignity, typical character, and monumental feeling. Alfred Stevens saw the importance of a certain formalism, and his little lion on the uprights of the outer railing of the British Museum remains unequalled, so far as I know, in modern work.[8]

The Hellenic race, the Greeks, whose art has had, and still possesses, such an influence over that of the modern world, while in their archaic period differing little in method of treatment and in use of ornament from the Asiatic races, the Assyrian and Egyptian and Persian, the elements of each of which they seemed to fuse and adapt, gradually developed a freer style, and, while never losing their monumental sense in sculpture, carried the human figure in sculpture to the greatest pitch of perfection. Their invention in purely ornamental forms was not conspicuous, nor was it needed, since they treated the human figure as their chief element in decoration. Their leading ornamental types may be traced to Asiatic prototypes—the palmette and the rosette, for instance. The scroll, perhaps, they may particularly claim to have developed, and the anthemion, from their primitive types.

This latter type of ornament, so generally used by the Greeks as a crest or crown upon their upright obelisk-like tombstones or steles, or to crest the angles of the pediments of their temples, is suggestive in its general form of a flame, or pair of wings.

LION, FORMERLY CRESTING THE OUTER RAILING OF
THE BRITISH MUSEUM. MODELLED BY ALFRED STEVENS,
AND CAST IN IRON.

GREEK STELE OR HEAD-STONE.

INDIAN (BRAHMAN)

FLAME HALO IN BRONZE SURROUNDING IMAGE OF THE GOD SIVA DESTROYING THE DEMON TRIPURASURA. (ZINC) FLAME HALO ENCLOSING IMAGE OF SURYA THE SUN GOD.

It is noteworthy that a similar form occurs, treated in detail in a variety of ways, as a glory or halo placed behind Buddhist images made in ancient India, Japan, and Burmah, often in carved wood and gilt metal or bronze, pierced and ornamented in a variety of ways—sometimes suggesting leafy trees, but generally radiating in their principal lines from a centre, like the anthemion. The flame was a sacred symbol with many ancient peoples, and it remains with us as the fitting emblem of inspiration.

PERSIAN POMEGRANATE FORMS (FROM A GOAT-HAIR CARPET, SOUTH KENSINGTON MUSEUM).

CELTIC ORNAMENT FROM A CROSS AT CAMPBELTOWN, ARGYLLSHIRE.

The gilded, almond-shaped glory inclosing the figure of the Virgin and of Christ in Gothic painting and sculpture seems to be another form of the same emblem, and a similar form is common in all Persian and Eastern ornament design. It generally appears as a kind of fruit or many-petaled flower, or flower and fruit combined. I am inclined to think that it may have originally had a religious significance associated with fire or life,[9] while its beauty of contour and adaptability in decoration of all kinds were sufficient to perpetuate it even if the original meaning were lost. If the Persians invented it, it might have had some reference to their own primitive fire-worship, while with the Arabs, and wherever the faith of Mohammed spread, it would still be significant of the prophetic fire, and it is certainly universally found in the ornament of Mohammedan countries. We might trace it back to its primitive form in the Assyrian tree of life, and this on the face of it seems its most likely source; and we find it in Persian work definitely taking the pomegranate form within the rayed leaves. The rayed flower or leaf form curiously reappears in a late Celtic cross in Argyllshire, in association with the characteristic knotted work, a kind of tree form, and filling of pattern carved in the stone and culminating in the cross.

Whatever race may really claim its invention or first effective use, it appeals now universally to the ornamental sense, and has become the common property of designers, who do not usually disturb themselves with the question whether they have stolen a fruit from the tree of life, or sacred fire from an unknown hearth, so long as they can fill a space effectively or make an attractive and adaptable design.

Another form, now no less universal, is probably Persian in origin, although it has found a settled home in India—I mean what is known as the Indian palmette, so familiar to designers for Manchester calico prints.

I am told by Mr. Purdon Clarke that this palm shape denotes benison or blessing, or a message of goodwill of some kind. This answers to the symbolical meaning of the palm in the Bible, as carried by benign and holy persons and angels. Here would be a symbolical reason for its longevity in ornament, as it would naturally commend itself to an eastern race in a sun-burnt land, to whom the suggestion of shady palms would always be grateful. But here, again, the beauty of its contour appeals to the ornamentist on independent grounds. He values it for its graceful mass in a pattern, for its bold and sweeping curves, for its value as an inclosing form for small floral fittings.

To the Persian and Hindu designers, with their exquisite and subtle sense of ornament, with their passion for elaborate intricacy, such a form as this is utilized to its utmost capacity, both in counter-balancing and superimposed masses upon flowery fields, and as inclosures for smaller fields of pattern; while the abundant flora of their spring-time blossoms in a new and translated existence in their richly patterned printed and woven textiles, and in the carved ornament of their buildings.

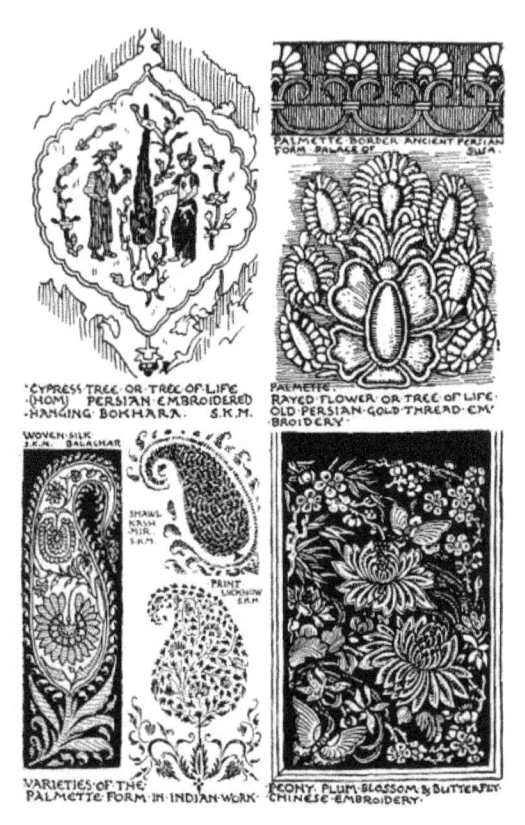

TYPICAL ORNAMENTAL FORMS IN PERSIAN, INDIAN, AND CHINESE DESIGNS.

The influence in Arabic ornament of the Mohammedan faith, too, in forbidding the representation of living forms, turned the ingenuity and invention of the Arabic and Eastern designer in a purely ornamental direction, and as a result we get extremely elaborate patterns, either purely geometric, or filling the interstices of a geometric framework in inlays and carved and pierced work. These patterns from the pulpit of a mosque at Cairo, now in the South Kensington Museum, work of the fourteenth and fifteenth centuries, show how fine and delicate Arabic ornament became. We may note the star-shape formed by the intersection of the lines. The star is an emblem of the Deity (Allah).

The plateaus and slopes of the Himalayas, which are the northern mountainous boundary of India, were supposed to be the cradle of that great wandering, colonizing, adaptive, speculative, and organizing race, the Aryans, from which we Western people, according to one theory, have sprung, dispersing over the world, and settling in different countries and climates. The race has greatly differentiated in speech, customs, and forms of art; and yet through them all it is rather differences in similarities, or similarities in differences, that we trace.

Latin, Teutonic, Celtic, suggest great divergences both in spirit and form, yet perhaps the correspondences are more frequent than the divergences. When we see how greatly members of the same family differ from one another in tastes and habits, can we wonder that members of the *greater* human family should be so different in tastes and habits, under different skies and conditions of life?

ARABIAN FOURTEENTH CENTURY CARVED AND INLAID PULPIT, CAIRO (SOUTH KENSINGTON MUSEUM. DRAWN BY W. CLEOBURY).

When we turn further east the difference seems greater, the gaps larger. The Mongolian race seems further apart and suggests a remoter antiquity. Their geographical remoteness and their persistent adhesion to their ancient customs seem to have fixed more or less of a gulf between them and the western peoples, and there is a corresponding contrast in the forms of their art. It is familiar, and yet remains strange; it has been constantly imported amongst us, and has more than once influenced European fashions in decorative design, as in the sixteenth and seventeenth centuries through the

Dutch, and in the last century in England in Chippendale furniture and porcelain, while China has given its name to the finer ware of the modern potter, of which it taught him the secret. To this day the willow pattern in blue upon plates and dishes, with its Chinese legend, scenery, and personages, remains a popular pattern, wonderfully little changed by its English translator. All the typical characteristics are found in its details, the typical Chinese house raised upon its first story of stone—with its bamboo trellises and quaintly curved tiled roof. The Chinese dragon remains a distinct breed, influencing here and there the form of the mythical beasts in design of other races, such as the Persian and Indian, but remaining as characteristically Chinese itself as the Pagoda.

ARABIAN FOURTEENTH CENTURY CARVED AND INLAID PULPIT, CAIRO (SOUTH KENSINGTON MUSEUM. DRAWN BY W. CLEOBURY).

The love of trellis-like backgrounds and diagonal diapers for floral designs is a very marked feature with the Chinese designer, and it suggests the native fantastic and ingenious bamboo constructions used in the framing and panelling of their dwellings and temples, dominated by that distinct love of quaintness and queerness which seems a part of the artistic sense in the yellow race, and is as marked as their love of bright colour and emphatic pattern.

Their formidable neighbours, relations, and rivals, the Japanese, exhibit in the art up to a certain stage much the same qualities and influences, their art indicating a gradual transformation in style from the primitive mythical and religious and symbolical towards the more domestic, familiar, and naturalistic. But before coming into contact with European forms of art they began to develop a naturalistic feeling in their art which in the present century has become the dominant note, and, joined with a certain inventive quaintness and ornamental reserve, has had so tremendous an influence upon the art of Europe, more especially modern French art.

Only about forty or fifty years ago Japan was practically in a mediæval condition, its arts and handicrafts in a most fertile and flourishing condition of living traditions; but that very quickness and alertness, that receptivity and artistic impressionableness which has enabled them to produce such a mass of wonderful work in so many branches of cunning craftsmanship, have exposed them to the modern European influences, which, however they may have, in the process of rapid assimilation, contributed to their material power as a nation in the modern capitalistic and industrial sense, have had most disastrous commercializing and deteriorating effects upon Japanese art and handicraft, leading to hasty work and cheap and gaudy production—merely to catch the demand.

PANEL IN CARVED AND INLAID WOOD FROM THE MOSQUE OF TOOLOON IN CAIRO. FOURTEENTH OR FIFTEENTH CENTURY SARACENIC.

Artistic and racial traditions, however, die hard. Even in Western Europe, in constant intercourse and intercommunication as we now are, and while international influence tends to soften and blend racial differences, and social relations to mix them, elements which differentiate the Teuton from the Latin, the Celt from the Saxon, still survive. In the process of the adoption of even the same ideas each race, each nation, gives a different interpretation to them, just as different individuals will give a different interpretation in drawing from the same model. The character is not changed by the new dress, and the dress becomes influenced by the wearer. Thus, in adopting ideas and forms of art, a new direction or character is developed owing to the racial instincts of the people adopting them.

German Renascence work, for instance, may be full of details, the forms of which come from Italy or Greece, but the combination and treatment, the application of them, become characteristically German—characteristically full of detail, and fantastic, with a tendency to be overloaded and restless, like their Gothic work. Such variations of the same type among different peoples may be likened to the variations of language in the same country, where the same language is spoken, but with a different accent.

It is this difference of *accent* now, under our complex modern life, which makes the chief difference in forms of art, and which betrays racial influence. The actual systems of building pattern, of pattern forms, methods of drawing and modelling figures, and the various handicrafts have all been discovered long ago, but it is in their recombination and adaptation—our interpretation and use of them, and in the power of variation and expression, that modern invention and predilection tell.

It would be interesting to endeavour to symbolize the fundamental racial characteristics and preferences by certain typical forms and colours in procession.

The races inhabiting the warm countries, southern and eastern, would be distinguished by emphatic contrasting colours and patterns. Just as the tiger owes his barred coat to his habit of hiding in coverts and jungles, where the bright sunlight falls through the tall grasses and palms in stripes; so where the contrast of light and shade is so sharp as in Africa, there appears to be a deeply-rooted preference for barred colours and striped patterns among the dark race, which they have carried with them to America, and which curiously reappears as a necessary part of the equipment of the sham Ethiopian serenader in our streets.

The black and white or red and white barred courses characteristic of Arabian and Moorish architecture have been alluded to before, and, though they have been used in other countries, they always suggest the country which seems to have given them birth.

Supposing, then, we wanted to express in a typical symbolical way the racial preferences and characteristics in ornamental art, a black and white barred shield and a palm might be appropriate pattern emblems for the African or the Moor; while the Egyptian would naturally bear a lotus and a scarabæus, with a winged globe for a standard; the Assyrian a tree of life; the Persian would bear the flame-shaped flower, and the device of Ormuzd and Ahrimanes contending for the mastery; the Indian would carry the palmette and a peacock, and would share with the Arab the geometric star-form and richly floriated robes; the Chinese would show the dragon blazon, and carry the peony; the Japanese the red disk of the rising sun, and a bough of plum blossom; the Turanian the crescent and the star; the Greek the anthemion, and the figure of Pallas Athene; the Roman an eagle standard, and an image of Mars; the Scandinavian a raven, and a runic knot. These might represent the ancient world of art. The modern and western races it would be more difficult to symbolize in so primitive and typical a manner, since all of them have borrowed so largely from the ancient sources, and are themselves composed of such mixed and complex elements.

Italian art could only be represented by a fusion of most of the foregoing elements and types, and would require a crowd of distinguished retainers in architecture, sculpture, painting, and all the arts of design; but perhaps she might bear a typical classical scroll for a standard, as the typical designer of that form of ornament in so many varieties, from Roman times downwards, that Italy may be said to have made the scroll form essentially her own.

Germany might follow, great in bold and brave heraldry, or with a Gothic accent in richly-scrolled mantling, and a redundant display of Renascence ornament.

France, as a more volatile Pallas Athene, might, perhaps, bear the wavering lamp of executive and imitative skill, and dramatic instinct in design.

Spain would look coquettishly under a fan, wrapped in faded embroidery, bearing the Alhambra, like a pendent jewel: while for England, what artistic emblems are left? Well, we have been described as inveterate colonists, even in art. We can only make up in a fancy costume of historic patchwork, beginning with fragments of Roman mosaic pavement, by way of sandals, Saxon and Norman hose, Gothic surcoat and body armour, a classical cloak, and a Victorian Queen Anne gable by way of headgear, and perhaps a banner of eclectic wall-paper or printed cotton.

For all that, and perhaps because of it in some measure—did we take art seriously as a nation, and make it really a natural and essential part of our life, as it is its final expression; should we determine to set our house in order, and make England again "merrie," strong in her own borders, self-supporting, and self-reliant, not suffering the natural beauty of our land or our historic monuments to be ruthlessly defaced, in the supposed interests of trade; putting our trust in the capacity of the people, rather than in the multiplication of machines; uniting hand and brain in our work, thinking more of the ends of life and less of the means, when the means of an ample, simple life shall be within the reach of every citizen, then, well—*then* we might fairly expect to win the palm of life, as of art, without despoiling the African.

CHAPTER VII.—OF THE SYMBOLIC INFLUENCE, OR EMBLEMATIC ELEMENT IN DESIGN

THE desire to express and to communicate ideas seems to have impelled man from the earliest, and lies at the root of all art.

While much early ornament, as we have seen, is traceable to a constructive origin, another kind, or another branch of the tree of design is traceable to a symbolic origin, and springs from the endeavour to express thought—to find a succinct language in which to express some sense of the great powers of nature, and their influence upon the daily life of man—to embody even in a pictorial emblem, symbol, or allegory his primitive conceptions of the order of the universe itself.

The mystery and wonders of nature absorbed the thoughts and touched the imagination of early as of later man, and primitive symbolic forms, or signs, constantly bear upon such ideas.

There is a symbolic sign (known to archæologists as the *fylfot* or *sauvastika*) of very simple form, which is found very widely scattered among the relics of many different races and early peoples. "It is found," says Dr. March (of the Lancashire and Cheshire Archæological Society, who has written very suggestively and learnedly on the subject), "on archaic Greek pottery, on the stamped clay of Swiss lake dwellings, adorning Latin inscriptions on Roman altars"; is common in India and Asia; is met with in Scandinavia, Iceland, Shetland, and Scotland; in Celtic Ireland, in Saxon England, as well as in Germany. The sign was adopted by Christians, is found in the catacombs of Rome, in the cathedrals of Winchester and Exeter, on a shield in the Bayeux tapestry, and on English mediæval brasses. It also occurs on a bell at Hathersage Church in Derbyshire, dated 1617.

This sign appears to have originally signified the supreme god of the Aryans, and became the emblem of the divinity from whom emanates the one movement of the universe; later, it may have merely indicated the axial rotation of the heavens round the Pole Star, and still later it was used simply as a benedictory sign or mark of good luck. When the feet were turned to the left the nocturnal movement of the stars was suggested, and when the feet turned to the right the diurnal movement of the sun was supposed to be indicated. The sign is frequently placed in a circle. A very few of its stages will suffice to show its transformation into ornament. We may thus see how a sign purely symbolical, used as we should use writing, becomes in course of time a decorative unit, and is incorporated into ornament. A kindred form is composed of three crescents, which has its heraldic descendant in the three armoured legs of the bearings of the Isle of Man. Here we seem to see the idea of rotation very emphatically conveyed.

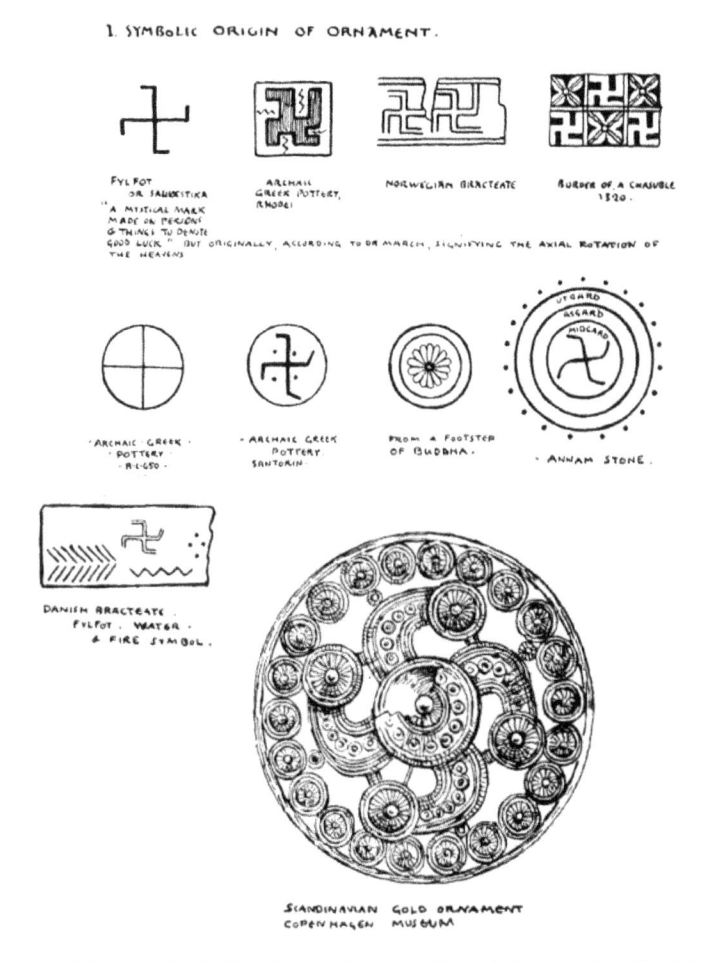

1. SYMBOLIC ORIGIN OF ORNAMENT.

The primitive symbols for fire and water found (as on the Danish *bracteate*) in association with the *fylfot* sign shown above, form linear patterns in themselves, and frequently recur in constructive and surface ornament; the former suggesting the method of setting the Roman bricks, called "herring bone," which constantly occurs in modern work in brick paving and wood parquet, forming one of the simplest and most satisfactory plans for floors and pavings in such materials.

POLYNESIAN ORNAMENT FROM HERVEY ISLAND PADDLE

The zigzag, as an ornament incised on clay vessels painted in patterns, or carved in masonry, has been a very favourite form from the ancient Egyptian decorators (to whom it possessed its original significance as water) onwards, becoming in later times more particularly characteristic of Scandinavian ornament and Romanesque architecture. The zigzag, however, appears to have an independent source and meaning in the evolution of Polynesian ornament. In the so-called "Paddles," decorated with carved patterns which are now considered to be really tables of descent, we may see rows of human figures arranged formally, the legs and arms bent. The angles thus formed, in the course of repetition and abbreviation, become simple lines of zigzag pattern.

The circle, a universal and important element in ornamental design of all times and kinds, appears early as a symbol for the sun. We might trace it from its primitive cross and disk and rayed ornament common to all primitive art to the splendid Greek conception of Phœbus Apollo in his chariot drawn by fiery horses, which figures so constantly in Greek design, the circular flaming disk being represented in the wheel, though in an early relief discovered by Dr. Schliemann the head of Apollo is surrounded by rays, which gives the type generally used by Gothic and modern designers in symbolic representations of the sun—simply a face in the circle surrounded by rays.

Another means of symbolical expression by the use of the circle is to be found in a type of Scandinavian ornament composed of three circles, one within the other, which with the rayed sun frequently occurs either singly, as in the form of a metal shield boss or a fibula, or as the unit of a repeating textile pattern, or as a border. An Anglo-Saxon lady in a Benedictional executed for St. Ethelwold at Winchester in the tenth century (963-984) wears a dress so decorated. The original symbolic meaning of this ornament is supposed to bear upon the Norsemen's conception of the universe, the inner circle, representing the *midgard*, or the earth; the second, the *osgard*, or *asgard*, the abode of the gods; and the *utgard*, the world beyond, inhabited by giants and spirits of evil. Beyond the outer circle is a circle of dots signifying stars. (See fig. on p. 224.)

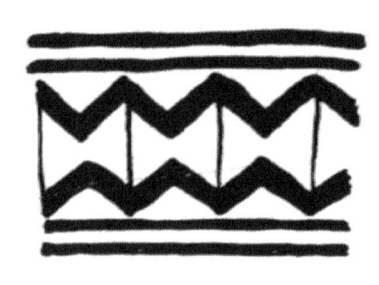

POLYNESIAN ORNAMENT. EVOLUTION OF THE ZIGZAG.

The old Norse sagas and the songs of Edda give the whole Norse scheme of the universe. "Igdrasil, the great ash tree of the universe of time and of life. The boughs stretched out into heaven, its highest point, and overshadowed Walhalla, the hall of the heroes. Its three roots reached down to dark Hel, to Jötunheim, the land of the Hrimthurses, and to Midgard, the dwelling-place of the children of men. The world-tree was ever green, for the fateful Norns sprinkled it daily with the water of life from the fountain of Urd, which flowed in Midgard. But the goat Heidrun, from whom was obtained the mead that nourished the heroes, and the stag Eikthyrnir browsed upon the leaf-buds, and upon the bark of the tree, while the roots down below are gnawed by the dragon Nidhögg and innumerable worms: still the ash could not wither until the last battle should be fought, where life, time and the world were all to pass away. So the eagle sang its song of creation and destruction on the highest branch of the tree."[10]

It is interesting to compare such a conception with the ancient Hindu idea of the world, which indeed may have been its original form as the earlier Aryan conception. There is no tree, but the great snake of time compasses all; the serpent with its tail in its mouth, an emblem of continuous time which still survives. Upon this rests the tortoise, which seems to correspond with the Norsemen's dragon, though here it may serve as the solid basis of the world. The world appears as a sort of dome in three tiers, reminding us of the Norsemen's three circles. This is supported upon the backs of three elephants, which seem here to fill the position of the Norns or the Fates.

The ash tree Igdrasil, the sustainer of the Norse universe, reminds one of the eastern tree of life—the tree of life of the garden of Eden, and the fountain of the rivers of the Asiatic paradise which, with the figures of Adam and Eve, the typical father and mother of the whole human race, have so constantly figured in art of all kinds, both eastern and western, and continue to stand in the midst of the garden in endless designs and pictures, surrounded by the birds and beasts, as the type and emblem of the origin of the world in the Christian cosmos.

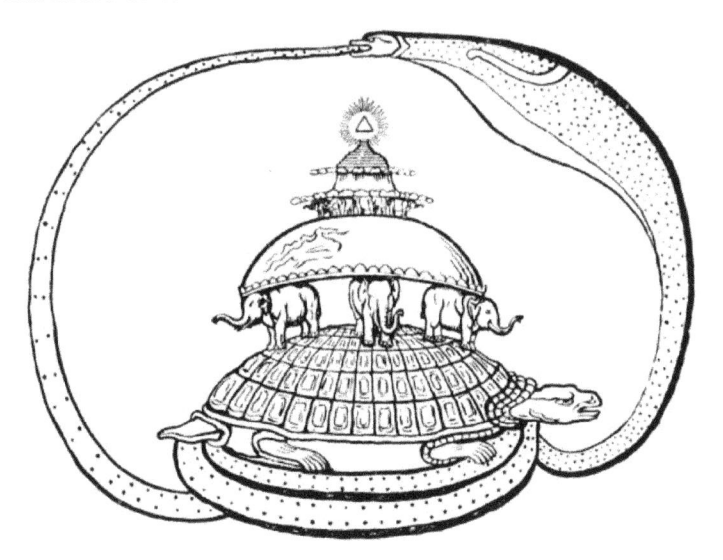

HINDU SYMBOL OF THE UNIVERSE.

The ancient Egyptians, whose art was almost entirely in the nature of a symbolic language, when they wished to express the divine creative power which sustains the universe, designed a winged globe encircled or upborne by two serpents—here we get, perhaps, the snake of time again. Sometimes the scarabæus, or sacred beetle, emblem of transformation and immortality, is represented covering an egg and supporting the sun, and they are the wings of the scarabæus which are given to the globe. This emblem is frequently carved over the gateways to their temples.

Then the Egyptians had an elaborate symbolism connected with death and the passage of the soul. The coffins and mummy cases are painted all over with symbolic devices, figures, birds, and animals having a sacred significance.

The soul is commonly represented as being borne in a boat, or barge, with curved stem and stern, terminating in lotus flowers. (The lotus symbolized new birth and resurrection.) The food for the journey is shown in the urns placed underneath the couch. Two mourners or watchers accompany it.

There is a copy of a large painting from Thebes in the British Museum showing the judgment of the soul; the Devourer, a monster part crocodile part hippopotamus, standing ready to devour the soul if the verdict is unfavourable. Further on the accepted soul appears before Osiris.

The goddess Nut (the heavens) is frequently painted upon the sarcophagi and mummy cases in the form of a seated or kneeling figure of a woman with very large wings outspread and curving upwards; she holds in her hands the feather—the symbol of power or domination. (We still speak of the feather in the cap.) She bears the disk of the sun upon her head. To the Egyptians, indeed, we owe the very embodiment of the mystery of existence itself—the sphinx who continues to propound her riddle afresh to every age.

EXAMPLES OF EGYPTIAN SYMBOLISM.

Greek mythology again, as exemplified in Greek art, expresses itself symbolically, and shows a gradual development from the primitive, ruder, and often savage personification of the powers of nature, more allied to the conceptions of the Northmen, to the idealized, refined, poetic and beautiful personifications of their later vase painting and Phidian sculpture. The symbolic intention and the personifying method was carried on and embodied in free and natural forms, though always governed by the ornamental feeling and necessities of harmonious relation to architectural and decorative conditions.

The first observers of the heavens, the primitive herdsman, hunter, the fisherman and the shepherd, have left their symbolic heraldry in the very stars above our heads; and Charles's or ceorls' wain and the signs of the zodiac still remind us of the primitive life of a pastoral and agricultural people.

The pediments of the Parthenon, for instance, are great pieces of symbolical art, and at the same time most beautiful as figure design and sculpture. It is distressing to think that so late as 1687 the Parthenon was practically complete as far as its sculpture and architecture. It was first used as a Greek Christian Church during the Middle Ages, and then, falling into the hands of the Turks, became a mosque; when the Venetians bombarded Athens in 1687 a shell dropped into the Parthenon, where the Turks had stored their powder, and blew out the whole centre of the building. Even in the broken and imperfect state in which we are now only able to see them, from the more or less complete figures and groups which compose its parts, we can gather an idea of the harmony and unity of the whole, and the complete union of the symbolism with the artistic treatment. The whole conception strongly appealed to the sentiment of the Athenian citizen, since the two pediments represented the contest of Athene and Poseidon for the patronage of Athens, arts and laws, or the rule of the sea. We all know that the arts and laws won, and that Athens is immortal by reason of her art and poetry and philosophy, not by her command of the sea. We modern English, perhaps, might do well to apply the lesson, and consider that after all it is not in mere appropriation of riches, extension of empire, material prosperity, or in our volume of trade, that the true greatness of a country consists, but in the capacity and heroism of her people.

In the eastern pediment the centre group expressed the birth of Athene herself, or rather her first appearance amongst the Olympians—the divine virgin deity and protectress of the city which bore her name, and whose colossal statue in ivory and gold stood on the Acropolis in front of the Parthenon. The other deities are grouped around, and on one side we have the Parcæ, the three fates controlling the life of man (which the Northmen embodied in the Norns); then, reclining at one side where the pediment narrows, the figure of the great Athenian hero, Theseus; and in the extreme angle the sun-god, Helios, with outstretched arms is seen guiding his horses, which emerge from the sea—being balanced at the corresponding angle by Selene, the moon, descending with her horses into the sea. Thus, we have a series of ideas expressed symbolically in heroic figures of deep import to the Athenians, and having also in the suggestion of the fateful control of human life, and the continuous order of nature in the rising sun and setting moon, a wide and lasting significance apart from the beautiful form and consummate art by which they are embodied.

The Parthenon stands high upon a rocky eminence, and from its western door you can see the blue Ægean Sea, the island of Salamis, and the harbour of Athens, the Piræus. Accordingly the sea-god Poseidon is sculptured upon the western pediment, with Cecrops, the first king and founder of Athens, with the queen. Another conspicuous figure there is the reclining figure of Ilissus, who represents the stream that flows around the western side of the Acropolis. The Greeks, and the Romans who borrowed from them, always symbolized a stream or a fountain by a reclining figure, half turned upon its side, and very frequently leaning upon an urn placed horizontally, from the mouth of which flows the wavy lines of water.

There is in the Vatican a Roman representation of the River Nile as a colossal reclining figure with long flowing hair and beard, like Zeus or Poseidon, holding a paddle. His tributaries being represented by a number of small Cupid-like boys, who clamber and play about him, or nestle at his side. The land of Egypt is typified by the sphinx upon which the figure leans.

Alinari Photo.]

IL NILO (VATICAN, ROME).

Father Thames has often figured in "Punch" depicted by John Tenniel as an old man with long hair and beard, not unlike his prototype, but somewhat degraded and worse for wear.

The Greek gods, too, and their Roman representatives were each distinguished by their proper and appropriate emblems, as well as by marked differences of character and physical type.

Chronos, or Time, afterwards Saturn, is always known by his scythe; Zeus or Jupiter, the Thunderer, by his thunderbolt; Poseidon or Neptune by his trident; Helios by his horses, and Apollo by his bow; Aphrodite or Venus by the golden apple won by the most beautiful; Pallas Athene, or the Roman Minerva, as goddess of the arts, by her serpent, her lamp, and her owl of wisdom; Artemis or Diana by the crescent moon; Hermes or Mercury by his *caduceus*—the serpent-twined staff, which has in modern times become an emblem of commerce—since Mercury was the messenger, the fetcher and carrier of the ancients, quick-witted and keen, and, according to some legends, not over scrupulous. His rod and serpents have reference to the story of his parting two snakes in combat, in which might be read a modern meaning of the individual gaining fortune through commercial competition, though that is not its usual signification. I only offer it as an example of reading a new meaning into an ancient symbol. Then, of course, Heracles or Hercules bears the apples of the Hesperides, or the Nemean lion's skin and his club. In the Hesperides story of the dragon-guarded tree of golden apples, and its three guardian sisters, we seem to have another form of the tree of life and the fates. An interesting Greek relievo in marble, enriched with mosaic in parts, at Wilton House, shows the Hesperidean tree with the apples, and twined with the guardian serpent, with Paris seated and Aphrodite approaching as if asking for the apple—the prize of the most fair.

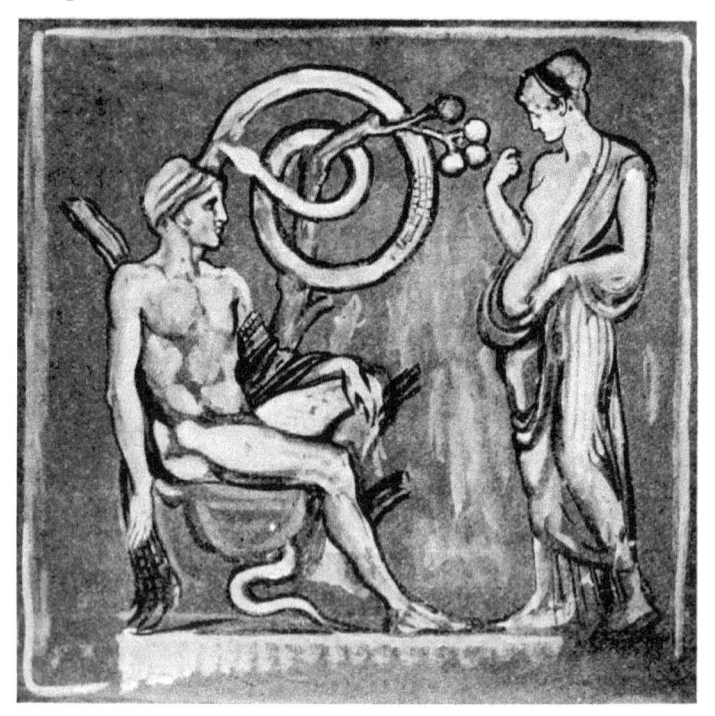

**VENUS AND PARIS. THE APPLES OF THE HESPERIDES.
FROM A RELIEF AT WILTON HOUSE.**

In the ancient Greek story of Pandora and her box—so suggestive a subject to artists, and fruitful in art—we have the classical version of the fall of man and origin of evil.

In the no less picturesque and poetical story of Persephone (or Proserpina), the daughter of Ceres, carried away by Pluto, the king of the underworld, darkness, and death, we have a beautiful allegory of the spring and the winter, since Persephone was allowed to return every year to the earth for a season, after she had eaten of the fatal pomegranate tree which grew in Pluto's garden.

One might multiply instances of the symbolic character of classical story and its symbolic embodiment in Greek and Roman art, but we must pass on to touch upon other sources and aspects of symbolism and emblem in art.

We know that many of our old fairy tales have a symbolical origin in ancient mythology, and have taken new and varied forms and local colours as they have travelled from their southern and eastern homes, and become naturalized in the art and literatures of different countries.

In such tales as "Jack and the Beanstalk" and "The Sleeping Beauty in the Wood," the climbing hero ascending the heavens to destroy the giant of darkness, in the first, the hero penetrating the darkness and awakening his destined bride from her enchanted sleep, in the second, for instance, the old solar mythology has been traced, and if we could trace the old folk tales back to their sources we might find them all related to primitive mythology or hero and ancestor worship. Thus do the spirits of the remote past sit at our firesides still, and kindle the imagination of our little folks: and in the rich tapestry of story and picture which each age weaves around it, elements from many different sources are continually and almost inextricably interwoven, as if the warp of human wonder and imagination was crossed with many coloured threads of mythological lore, history and allegory, symbolism and romance.

The early Christians, no less than the pagans, felt the necessity for symbols of their faith; and while at first borrowing considerably, and incorporating in their art forms belonging to the other faith they were supplanting, gradually, with the rise of power and influence, emblems more peculiarly belonging to an expression of the Christian ideal were adopted, or underwent considerable transformation. The design met with in the mosaics of the sixth century at Ravenna, the mausoleum of Galla Placidia, of the two stags drinking from a fountain, embodying the Psalmist's verse beginning, "As the hart panteth for the water brooks," although from the imagery of the older Scriptures, became an emblem of Christianity. The peacock appears, too, in Byzantine art, carved upon stone sarcophagi as an emblem of immortal life, either from the many eyes its feathers always open, or more probably because the eye feathers are shed and renew themselves every year. The vine, too, appears constantly as a Christian emblem, although with the Greeks it was sacred to Dionysos, and represented to them the divine, life-giving earth-spirit continually renewing itself, and bringing joy to men.

Although the symbolic use no less than the decorative beauty of winged figures had long ago been recognized, as Asiatic, Egyptian, and Greek art show, yet the Christian angel, both in its refined, half-classical form, as developed by the early Italian painters and sculptors from the thirteenth century onwards, and in northern Gothic work, became a distinct and beautiful type in art. In the work of Fra Angelico and Benozzo Gozzoli the angel figures are especially lovely.

Alinari Photo.]

CHRISTIAN EMBLEM. STAGS DRINKING (MAUSOLEO DI GALLA PLACIDIA, RAVENNA).

Alinari Photo.]

CHRISTIAN EMBLEM. PEACOCKS AND VINE. SARCOPHAGUS (ST. APOLLINARE IN CLASSE, RAVENNA).

Brogi Photo.]
FRA ANGELICO. ANGEL (UFFIZI, FLORENCE).

Brogi Photo.]
FRA ANGELICO. ANGEL (UFFIZI, FLORENCE).

No less distinct in its grotesqueness was the mediæval devil, although its origin was very probably the satyr of ancient classical art. The Roman satyr, with goat-legs and hoofs, bearded head, horns, and tail, furnishes, in fact, a very close prototype; and, being banned long ago as pagan when Christianity was in hand-to-hand conflict with paganism, would be sufficient to associate such a form with evil. There are some fiends represented in Orcagna's fresco, "The Triumph of Death," which are quite satyr-like, despite talons and bats' wings. Although with the Greeks the great god Pan is a mild and gentle deity enough, and though of the earth earthy, in a sense, yet as symbolical of spontaneous nature, and simple animal existence, piping on his reeds by the riverside, he always remains a favourite with the poet and the artist. Signorelli, for instance, in a beautiful picture (which our National Gallery somehow missed the opportunity of acquiring), gives a fine presentment of him.

It is interesting to compare the mediæval embodiments of evil with the ancient Persian symbolical representation of a combat of a king with a griffin, which may represent the conflict of Ormuzd and Ahrimanes as the typical principles or embodied powers of good and of evil.

Alinari Photo.]

ORCAGNA. FIENDS FROM "THE TRIUMPH OF DEATH" (FRESCO. CAMPO SANTO, PISA).

The creature (representing evil) is winged, and has birds' claws for its hind feet (like Orcagna's fiends), and lions' paws for its fore feet, the body of an ox or horse, the beak of an eagle or griffin, in some instances, in others it appears with a bull's head, and is certainly suggestive of power and terror.

The favourite Greek conception of the centaur, too, is an expressive symbolic embodiment of animal force, and the mythical sculptural combat in the metopes of the Parthenon is again suggestive of the conflict between the higher and the lower elements of human nature.

Returning again to Christian art, we find the image of the lamb, with the banner of the cross, was the badge of the Templar; and we find abundant symbolism in the various emblems and attributes of the apostles, saints, and martyrs, distinguished by the various emblems of their evangel, conversion, or martyrdom. The mystic symbols of the four evangelists are well known to every ecclesiastical designer—the angel of St. Matthew, the lion of St. Mark, the bull of St. Luke, the eagle of St. John.

The winged lion of St. Mark has become the distinguishing badge of the city of Venice, since the evangelist was supposed to be buried in the great church dedicated to his name. Its image in bronze upon the column in the Piazza impresses itself upon the eye and imagination of every visitor, while upon the companion columns we see the patron saint of the ancient republic—St. Isidore, with the crocodile. Placed there in 1329, the statue recalls the early days of Venice, and suggests its connection with the East.

COMBAT OF KING WITH GRIFFIN ANCIENT PERSIAN SCULPTURE PERSEPOLIS.

From Perrot & Chipiez Hist of Ancient Art in Persia after Flandrin & Coste.

Now national heraldry is often derived from the bearings of families or chiefs. Of such is our royal standard with its Plantagenet leopards and red lion of the Scottish kings. Though in the Irish harp we seem to get a purely national emblem, strictly speaking it is the heraldic bearing of one of the four provinces—Leinster.

These heraldic bearings and badges had their origin in very remote times, and take us back to earliest forms of human society, to the gens, and the tribe, who named themselves after some animal or plant, and adopted it as the distinguishing mark and ensign of the family to which they belonged, or to such primitive times as we read of in Mr. William Morris's "Roots of the Mountains" and "House of the Wolfings," where he speaks of "The House of the Steer" and "The House of the Raven." The distinguishing badges would be carved or painted over the porch, and borne upon the shield of the chief and the banner in battle.

In feudal times the practice was continued until family heraldry, owing to intermarriage, became very complicated, and family shields much quartered.

Distinctness and definite characterization of form were highly necessary, since in battle it was important to distinguish your enemies from your friends, and the banner of the chieftain, the knight, or king, would be the rallying point for their followers and retainers.

Heraldry became regulated by strict rules, and is now called a science, though its vitality and meaning have departed, except in an antiquarian and archæological sense. It has, however, a certain decorative value to the designer, as illustrating the principle of counterchange of colours, and from the heraldry of the mediæval period much may be learned in point of decorative treatment.

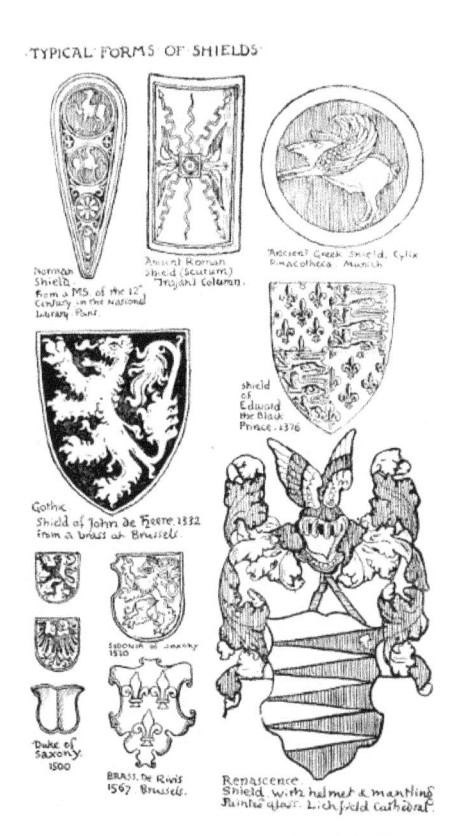

TYPICAL FORMS OF SHIELDS:

Norman Shield. From a MS. of the 12th Century in the National Library, Paris.
Ancient Roman Shield (Scutum) Trajan's Column.
Ancient Greek Shield. Cylix Pinacotheca. Munich
Gothic. Shield of John de Heere, 1332, from a brass at Brussels.
Shield of Edward the Black Prince, 1376.
Duke of Saxony, 1500.
SIDONIA of Saxony, 1510.
BRASS. De Rivis, 1567, Brussels.
Renascence Shield, with helmet & mantling Painted glass, Lichfield Cathedral.

The shield itself varies considerably in form. There is the round shield of the ancients used both by Greeks and Norsemen. This with the Greeks had pieces cut out at the sides sometimes. There was also a moon-shaped shield, similar in form to the shield used by our old invaders the Danes. Then we get the parallelogram, kite-shaped and oval shields of the Romans; the kite-shaped shield of the Normans; the lancet pointed shield, cut square at the top, of the first crusades. The Gothic shield becomes more variously hollowed and shaped with the development of plate armour, and in the fifteenth century frequently has a space cut out on the outer edge to allow of the tilting lance of the knight passing through without interfering with the guard. In Renascence times there was a revival of classical and fanciful forms in shields, and a return to its original form in the escutcheon, the term being derived from the Latin (*cutis*) word for skin or hide, which covered the ancient shields: but with the use of fire-arms shields declined, until the small steel buckler for the short-sword became its last working representative.

The character and the art of heraldic devices varies very much according to these changes in methods of warfare, and was also affected by the state of the arts generally.

We have only to compare the bold and frank heraldry of the thirteenth and fourteenth centuries with the coach-painter's heraldry of the present to realize the great change in feeling. Compare a Plantagenet lion with a Victorian one, a mediæval griffin with a nineteenth century specimen.

SICILIAN SILK TISSUE. TWELFTH CENTURY (SOUTH KENSINGTON MUSEUM).

The Gothic heraldic designer felt he must be simple and bold for the sake both of distinctness and ornamental effect. He emphasized certain features of his animals: he insisted very much, for instance, upon the claws of the lion, its mane and tail, its open mouth and tongue; in short, he felt it was his first business to make a bold and striking pattern, and whatever the forms of his heraldry, they were controlled by this feeling.

Heraldic devices formed a large part of the ornamental design of the Middle Ages in all kinds of materials. They were abundantly used in dress patterns and in hangings and textiles of all kinds. In the beautiful Sicilian silk stuffs, for instance, a leading feature of the repeat often consists of an emblematic or heraldic device of animals or birds, which give character and agreeable massiveness to the pattern.

Mediæval brasses afford many beautiful examples of heraldic treatment. Indeed, for ornamental feeling, expressed by very simple means and under very limited conditions, those of the thirteenth, fourteenth, and fifteenth centuries afford beautiful instances, which may be most profitably studied by designers of all kinds. Mr. Creeny's book on the Continental brasses may be recommended as containing many very beautiful examples from his own rubbings, notably from Belgium. Two specimens are given in Chapter VIII.

EX BELLO PAX, (From Alciati's "Emblems," 1522.)

But the love of symbol and emblem did not expire with the vigour of heraldic design. Indeed, a certain impetus was given to it by the invention of printing, which, diverting it into another channel, seemed to give it fresh life in association with literature. The sixteenth century was remarkable for its love of allegory and emblem, which was no doubt stimulated by the opening up of the stores of classical lore at the Renascence, and by the general stir and activity of thought of a time of transition, when new and old ideas were in conflict or in process of fusion. Life was full of variety, contrast, hope, fear, strife, love, art, romance and poetry, learning and the beginnings of scientific discovery. Out of the seethings of such elements, joined with the relics of mediæval *naïveté* and quaintness, came into existence the emblem book, which offered compact pictorial epigrams, by means of the woodcut and the printing press, to fit every phase of human life, thought, and vicissitude.

Holbein's "Dance of Death" was really a book of emblems, and the subject was a favourite one with the German sixteenth century designers. Very ancient ideas reappeared in these books, unearthed by scholars, from all sorts of sources, from the ancient Egyptians onwards. Such designs as those of the pelican feeding its young from its own breast, and the stork carrying its parent on its back, constantly reappear; and also the bees making their hive in a helmet, with the motto *Ex bello pax*, which reminds one of Samson's riddle of sweetness and strength.

FORTUNE, (From Alciati's "Emblems," 1522.)

The device of the crab, too, with a butterfly between its claws, and the motto *Festina lente*—hasten slowly—is a favourite. The phœnix, also, borrowed from ancient Egypt, but nowadays generally associated with life insurance. Fortune, with the sail of a ship standing on a globe, and sometimes a wheel, floating in a tempestuous sea, to express her fickleness and uncertainty, often appears. The fate of Ambition, in the fable of

Phaeton falling from Apollo's car; the snake in the grass—*Latet anguis in herba*; labour in vain, a man pouring water into a sieve, the sieve held by blindfold Love, also figures; the ass loaded with dainties and rich food, but stooping to eat the thistle by the wayside, appears as a symbol of Avarice. Æsop's fables were utilized, and classical mythology, in fact all was fish to the moral net of the emblem designer, and the multiplication of such collections in printed books is evidence of the moralizing, philosophizing tendency of the times, and the love of personifying and imaging ideas.

AMBITION, (From Alciati's "Emblems," 1522.)

AVARICE, (From Alciati's "Emblems," 1522.)

Elaborate designs, such as one of Romeyn de Hooghe (1670)—following the tablet of Cebes, B.C. 390, or the Latin version of 1507—allegorizing human life as a whole, from birth to death, under the device of a labyrinth or maze, with figures wandering about in its walks, under different influences, down to simple devices like the moth and the candle, are comprehended in these emblem books; but it is only reducing to small compass and to compact, portable, and popular form the same spirit of quaint invention which covered the walls and ceilings of great houses and public halls and tapestries with personifications, like the splendid series of the "Triumphs" of Petrarch, Love, Time, Death, and Chastity in our National Museum at South Kensington, as well as endless embodiments of the seasons, the senses, the virtues, and the vices. Emblematic art, however, like heraldry, became overlaid with pedantry, and its artistic interest died when its form became prescribed, and precedent and rule took the place of original invention.

The chief scope for symbol and emblem in our time lies in the province of decorative design, which in its highest forms may be regarded as the metre or poetry of art. The designer, like the poet, rejoices in certain limitations, which, while they fix and control his form and treatment, leave him extraordinary freedom in dealing suggestively with themes difficult or impossible to be approached in purely naturalistic form.

It is true we find emblematic art in very stiff and degraded forms, and applied to quite humdrum purposes. It is largely used in commerce, for instance, and one may find classical fable and symbolism reduced to a trade mark or a poster. Still trade marks, after all, fill the place, in our modern commercial war, of the old knightly heraldry—shorn of its splendour and romance, certainly—and given trade marks and posters they might as well be designed, and would serve their purpose more effectively if they were treated more according to the principles of mediæval heraldry, since they would gain at once character, distinctness, and decorative effect.

Allegorical art has, too, a modern popular form in the region of political satire and caricature, often potent to stir or to concentrate political feeling. This is almost a distinct province, to which many able and vigorous artists devote their lives and show their invention in the effective way in which the political situation is put into some piece of familiar symbolism which all can recognize and remember.

In the region of poetic design symbolism must always hold its place. When the artist desires to soar a little above the passing moment to suggest the past, to peer into the future; when he looks at human life as a complete whole, and the life of the race as an unbroken chain; when he would deal with thoughts of mans origin and destiny, of the powers and passions that sway him, of love, of hope and fear, of the mystery of life and nature, the drama of the seasons, he must use figurative language, and seek the beautiful and permanent images of emblematic design.

CHAPTER VIII.—OF THE GRAPHIC INFLUENCE, OR NATURALISM IN DESIGN

"THE graphic influence!" my readers may exclaim, "what existence has design apart from this, since the depicting power with whatever pencil, brush, modelling tool, chisel, pen is by its very nature bound up with it?"

That is quite true, yet for all that there is discernible a very distinct line of cleavage in art, a distinction of spirit and aim which seems to have divided or characterized artists and epochs from the very earliest.

I have often alluded to the drawings of the prehistoric cave men. These graphic outlines of animals, although generally incised upon the handles of weapons, always appear to me to indicate the purely naturalistic aim as distinct from the ornamental sense, as if the first object of the primitive artist had been to get as exact a profile as possible of the animals he knew; just as a modern artist, with superior facilities of pencil and paper, might make sketches at the Zoological Gardens without any idea of making them parts of a decorative design. The main difference seems to be that in purely graphic or naturalistic drawing individual characteristics or *differences* are sought for, while in ornamental or decorative drawing typical forms or *correspondences* are sought for.

PREHISTORIC GRAPHIC ART OF THE CAVE MEN.

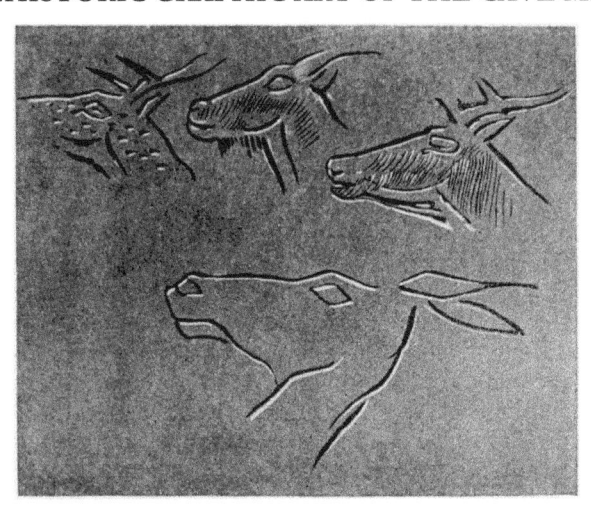

PREHISTORIC GRAPHIC ART OF THE CAVE MEN.

In the course of the development of historic art in different countries and among different peoples, under different social and political systems, we may yet discern a kind of strife for ascendency between these two principles, which still divide the world of art; and though in the most perfect art the two are found reconciled and harmonized, as being really two sides of the same question, the general feeling for art seems to swing from one side to the other, like the tides in ebb and flow. At one time human feeling in art seeks to perpetuate types, symbols, and emblems of the wonder of life and the mysteries of the universe, as in the art of ancient Egypt. At another its interest is absorbed in the representation of individual characteristics and varieties, striving to follow nature through her endless subtleties and transformations, as in our own day; when the different aims inspiring our artists might be set down as—

(1) The desire to realize, or to represent things as they *are*.

(2) The desire to realize, or to represent things as they *appear* to be.

Under whatever differences of method or material, I believe it will be found that this real difference of mental attitude behind them accounts for the varieties we see, that is to say, in any genuine and thoughtful work.

Every sincere artist naturally desires to *realize* his conception to the best of his ability, in the most harmonious and forceful way; but in the course of the development of a work of art of any kind there are problems to be solved at every turn.

Is it a piece of repeating surface ornament we are designing? We feel we must subordinate parts to the whole, we must see that our leading structural lines are harmonious, we cannot emphasize a bit of detail without reference to the total effect. We may find the design wants simplifying, and have to strike out even some element of beauty. Such sacrifices are frequently necessary. Our love of naturalism may induce us to work up our details, our leaves and flowers, to vie with natural appearance in full light and relief, until we find we are losing the repose and sense of quiet planes essential to pattern work, and getting beyond the capacities of our material, so that we may realize that even skill and graphic power may be inartistic if wrongly applied or wasted in inappropriate places.

Is it a landscape we desire to transcribe or express upon paper or canvas? Sun and shadow flit across it, changing every moment dark to light and light to dark, so that the general emphasis and expression of the scene constantly vary, like the expression of a human face, as we watch it. Which shall we choose? Which seems the most expressive, the most beautiful? Again, shall we content ourselves with a general superficial impression, leaving details vague? Shall we aim at truth of tone, or truth of local colour? Shall we dwell on the lines of the composition? Shall we spend all our care upon getting the planes right, or rely for our main interest upon light and shade and delicate definition of detail?

All these different problems belong to graphic representation of nature, to graphic methods of drawing and design, and the work of different artists is distinguished usually by the way in which they seem to feel—the particular aspect or truth on which they mostly dwell in their work.

Even the most abstract symbolic or ornamental drawing in pure outline must have some graphic quality, though intentionally limited to the expression of few facts.

The method by which an ancient Egyptian painter or hieroglyphic carver blocked out a vulture or a hawk, relying either solely on truth of mass or silhouette, or on outline and emphatic marking of the masses of the plumage, or the salient characteristics, such as claws and beak, although extremely abstract, was full of natural truth and fact as far as it went, and left no doubt as to the birds depicted.

Egyptian Treatment of Birds (from painted Mummy Cases, British Museum)

Something of the same kind of quality is found in Japanese drawings of birds, with less severity and monumental feeling. The graphic or naturalistic feeling is strongest and the individual accidents are dwelt upon. In modern European natural history drawings of birds and animals, we often lose this bold graphic sense of character in the general aspect, while small superficial details of plumage and textures are carefully attended to. There is often less life though actually more likeness. The general tendency in the development of the art of a people seems to have been from the formal, monumental, and symbolic type of representation and design in strict relation to architectural structure and decoration, towards freer naturalism, individual portraiture, and a looser graphic style.

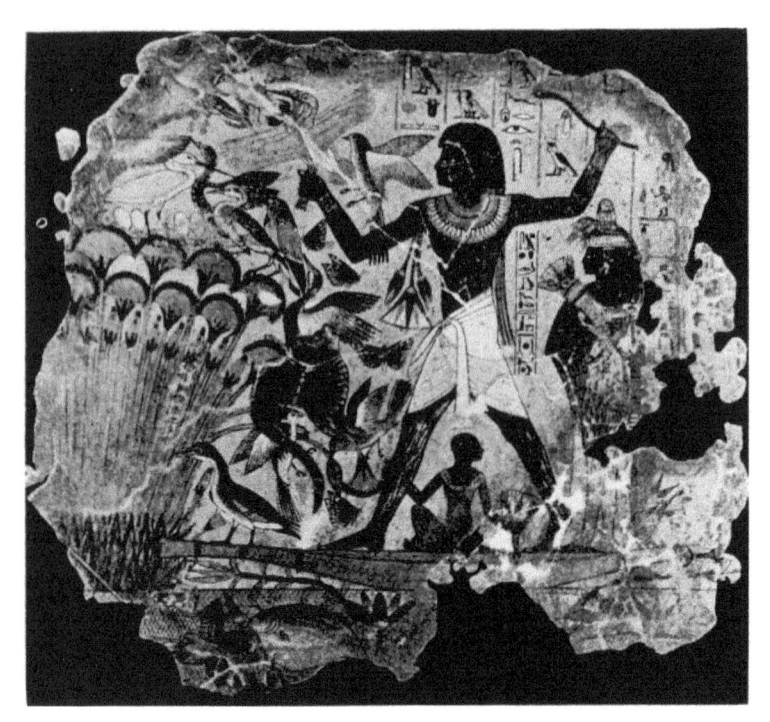

A FOWLER. WALL PAINTING. NINETEENTH DYNASTY (BRITISH MUSEUM).

We may trace this tendency even in the strictly monumental and stereotyped art of ancient Egypt, which notably in the portrait sculpture even of the ancient empire is remarkable for extraordinary realism; and in the wall paintings of the later period of the Theban empire (as in the tomb of Beni Hasan), which show considerable freedom and vitality.

JAPANESE GRAPHIC ART. FROM "THE HUNDRED BIRDS OF BARI."

JAPANESE GRAPHIC ART. FROM "THE HUNDRED BIRDS OF BARI."

A most notable example of realism is the famous "Scribe" in the Louvre, a coloured statuette, believed to date from the fifth or sixth dynasty, of extraordinary vitality. The eyes consist of an iris of rock crystal, surmounting a metal pupil, and set in an eyeball of opaque white quartz.

Greek sculpture, again, shows a gradual development from the archaic period, in which it resembles early Asiatic art, up to the refinement, freedom, and beauty of design of the Phidian period, when the balance between naturalistic feeling and monumental feeling appears to have been perfect. Then later, as the result of a desire for more obvious naturalism and dramatic expression, we get quite a different feeling in the sculptures of the frieze of the great altar at Pergamos, which represents the strife of the gods and the Titans—a tremendous subject, worked out with extraordinary power, skill, and learning in alto relievo; but despite the energy and dramatic movement, after the delicacy and reposeful beauty of the Parthenon sculptures, we feel that these qualities have been gained at a considerable cost and loss; but it is interesting as representing the more realistic and dramatic side of Greek art.[11]

EGYPTIAN SCRIBE. PORTRAIT STATUETTE. FIFTH OF SIXTH DYNASTY (LOUVRE).

But the grace and charm of Greek art never seemed really to die out. All the best Roman art was inspired by it, if not actually carried out by Greek artists; and, owing to Greek colonies, Greek traditions had long been naturalized in Italy, where they found a congenial soil. Fine portrait sculpture was done in the imperial period—as the Augustus and the head of Julius Cæsar and many other well-known busts testify. Also the truth and beauty of some of their animal sculpture we may see in the fine style of the frieze of sacrificial animals discovered in 1872 in the Forum. We seem to see the Greek spirit in the decorative splendour of the Byzantine period, and again, in Italian dress, inspiring the painters and sculptors of the early Renascence, in the work of Giotto, Ghiberti, and Donatello for instance. With the development of Gothic architecture in the thirteenth century a new and distinct feeling for naturalism arose, which influenced through architecture all the arts of design. In fact, all through the Gothic period design seems to have had more the character of a vital organic growth, controlled by a certain tradition and the influence of architectural style, yet within these limits and those of the material of its expression developing an extraordinary freedom both of invention and graphic power, which culminated at the end of the fifteenth century, or was perhaps absorbed by the classicism of the Renascence. Thirteenth century Gothic sculpture at its best, as we find it in France, has almost the simplicity, grace, and natural feeling of Greek work. This may be seen in the figures from the west front of Auxerre Cathedral, and also in the porch of Amiens; and in the portrait effigies of this period and onwards through the three centuries in those of our own cathedrals and churches we find abundant evidence of graphic power in careful and characteristic portraiture, united with beauty of design in detail and decorative effect.

SCULPTURED FRIEZE DISCOVERED IN THE FORUM, 1872.

SCULPTURE FROM AUXERRE CATHEDRAL. THIRTEENTH CENTURY.

SCULPTURE FROM AMIENS CATHEDRAL. FOURTEENTH CENTURY.

What we should call realism comes out wonderfully in the treatment of the statue of St. Martha at St. Urbain, Troyes, a work of the fifteenth century.

Gothic art, too, was a familiar art, intimate and sympathetic with human life in all its varieties.

In the beautiful illuminated Psalters, Missals, Books of Hours, and chronicles of the Middle Ages, the life of those days is presented in bright and vivid colours. We see the labourers at work in the fields, ploughing, sowing, reaping, threshing, treading the wine-press. We see the huntsman, the fisherman, and the shepherd; the scribe at his work, the saint at his prayers, the knight at arms. The splendour and pomp of jousts and tournaments, with all their bright colour and quaint heraldry; we see the king in his ermine, and the beggar in his rags, the monk in his cell, the gallant with his lute—delicate miniatures often set in burnished gold, and adorned with open fret-work or borders of flowers and leaves.

These borders in course of time from a purely fanciful ornamental character become real leaves, flowers or fruit, as in the Grimani Breviary, attributed to Memling, the famous Flemish painter, where the borders are in some pages naturalistic paintings of leaves and berries, birds and butterflies, on gold grounds with cast shadows. Here we get the naturalistic feeling dominating again and the pictorial skill of the miniaturist triumphing, but the effect is still rich and ornamental.

When the printing press in the middle of the fifteenth century began to rival the scribe with his manuscript, it offered in the woodcut a new method to the artist, which led to a new development of graphic power and design by means of line and black and white, though at first intended merely as a method of furnishing the illuminator with outlined designs as book illustrations and ornaments to be filled in with colour and gold.

ST. MARTHA (ST. URBAIN, TROYES).

MEMLING. "DELIVERANCE OF ST. PETER" (GRIMANI BREVIARY).

MEMLING. "DAVID PLACING THE ARK IN THE TABERNACLE"

(GRIMANI BREVIARY).

The black and white effect, however, grew to be liked for its own sake: not only was it found to afford a considerable range of decorative effect by different treatment of line and solid black, but the graphic designer found in the rich vigorous woodcut line a suggestive and emphatic means of expression. The best artists of the time gave themselves to the work, and notably in Germany, the home of the invention of printing itself. Cologne, Mainz, Augsburg, Ulm, Nuremberg were all famous centres of activity in the printer's art, as well as Venice and Florence, Basle and Paris.

Up to the end of the fifteenth century the Gothic and ornamental feeling is still dominant in the treatment of the design of woodcuts in books, and most instructive and suggestive they are in simplicity of method and line, and directness of expression.

Characteristic German work of Gothic feeling and considerable graphic force is seen in the woodcuts of the Nuremberg Chronicle (1493) designed by Michael Wolgemuth, the master of Albert Dürer. In these vigorous cuts we may plainly see the tradition of that Gothic feeling and style of graphic design afterwards developed in the work of the great German designer.

The splendid woodcuts of Dürer's "Apocalypse," and of the "Little Passion," and the design called "The Cannon" (1518), give us further insight into his method of drawing and his graphic power; and one can hardly go to stronger or better examples for the study of expression by means of bold line work, a command of which is most valuable to designers in all materials, though, of course, especially so to those who desire to make black and white drawing their principal pursuit. For Dürer's finer line treatment on copper there is no better example than the portrait of Erasmus.

ALBERT DÜRER. "THE APOCALYPSE."

ALBERT DÜRER. PORTRAIT OF ERASMUS, 1526.

ALBERT DÜRER. "THE CANNON," 1513.

The style of drawing shown in these woodcuts was no doubt to a great extent determined by the nature of the method of cutting the block. The drawing on the smooth plank—not on the cross section of the tree, as in modern wood-engraving—was actually cut with a knife, not a graver. Each line had to be excavated, as it were, from the surface, the ground or white part sunk each side, so as to make it take the ink and print the impression of its surface sharply upon the paper in the press. These conditions would necessarily lead to a certain economy of line both as to quantity and direction, and would favour the use of bold outline and lines expressive of relief surfaces or shadow arranged in a comparatively simple way, and often running into solid black, as in small folds of drapery and details. The drawing was probably done with a reed or quill pen, which latter still remains perhaps the best tool for emphatic, graphic drawing on the scale of book designs, since it offers the maximum possibility of effect with the minimum of simplicity and economy of means. Its only rival (though it may also be regarded as a useful auxiliary to the pen) is the narrow flexible brush point, and this has the advantage of spreading more easily into solid blacks, though more likely to lead one into looseness of style owing to its very facility.

Fine and firm graphic draughtsmanship and rich design, with a fine sense of the decorative value of armorial bearings and processional grouping, may be seen in the famous series of woodcuts called "The Triumphs of Maximilian," in which Albert Dürer and Hans Burgmair co-operated. That is to say each did a large proportion of the designs. It was a very vast work for wood-engraving. The scheme was in two parts, one consisting of a design of a triumphal arch, in general idea in emulation of the old Roman imperial triumphal arches. This part of the work consisted of ninety-two blocks which, when put together, form one woodcut 10½ feet high by 9 feet wide. This part was all designed and drawn upon the blocks by Albert Dürer, and engraved by Hieronymus Andreæ.

ALBERT DÜRER. "LITTLE PASSION." THE TAKING DOWN FROM THE CROSS.

HANS BURGMAIR. GROUP OF KNIGHTS FROM "THE TRIUMPHS OF MAXIMILIAN."

The second part consisted of the triumphal procession and the triumphal car of Maximilian and his Queens, designed by Dürer, as well as other allegorical and heraldic cars and warlike machines, and cars with officers of the court, groups of knights in armour, men-at-arms of all kinds, country people, and even groups of African savages. Sixty-six of the designs of the procession are due to Hans Burgmair.

It is noteworthy that the general scheme for this triumph was first painted on large sheets of parchment, which still exist in the Imperial Library at Vienna; and the woodcuts followed this more or less in design, Dürer's drawings being a freer rendering, while Burgmair's are supposed to keep more closely to the painted scheme of the miniaturists, though it is quite possible they may both have furnished sketches for the miniaturists' version also. This great undertaking, however, was never finished, and its progress came to an end with the death of the emperor in January, 1519. The work was supposed to have been commenced in 1512.

For more purely ornamental effect in black and white the rich, bold, yet sensitive outline of the Venetian and Florentine woodcuts should be studied, and their use of solid black.

The amount of graphic expression and even of statement of natural fact which can be put into pure outline alone is, of course, enormous.

The value of the graphic illustrative capacity of the woodcut was soon discovered and utilized by the writers of natural histories and compilers of Herbals of the early days of printing onwards.

There is a beautiful Herbal written by Dr. Fuschius (whose name we seem to have perpetuated in the Fuchsia). It was printed at Basle in 1542, and the drawings are fine examples of what outline can do, and remarkable for a combination of beautiful style united with natural truth and decorative feeling. One of the horned poppy is here given. The book is also interesting in the portraits of the draughtsmen and wood-engraver, or *formschneider*, given at the end.

The woodcuts of the plants given in the Herbal of Matthiolus, where more lines of surface and shadow are introduced, are vigorous and good, full of style and character, and expressive of the salient facts of growth. The same may be said of those in our own Gerard's Herbal, though the impressions are not generally so bright or good; but then it was produced during the decline of the printer's art, in the later years of the sixteenth century.

Though used for purely illustrative purposes, much as the cuts put into modern dictionaries to make certain facts clear to the mind, these woodcuts have always, over and above fidelity to the main facts of growth and character, a sense of design. They are not merely drawings of plants, but they are well put together as panels or spaces of design, and effectively though unobtrusively ornament the page.

For expressive and sensitive line and touch in the rendering of flowers, the Japanese artists are remarkable, and their books, printed from wood-blocks cut on the plank in the old European way, are full of spirit and suggestiveness. Drawn on the wood with a pointed brush, which is occasionally spread to yield solid black, or turned sideways, or dragged, to vary the quality of the line, they show that extreme ease and facility in the expression of form by simple means which only long practice, direct work, and intimate knowledge and close observation of nature could produce. The added flat and delicate tints of colour enhance the effect and give them a decorative beauty entirely their own, though planned in the spaces they occupy in a totally different spirit from the old Herbal woodcuts we have been considering. They belong in the main rather to the second point of view or artistic impulse in art, which I characterized at the beginning as the desire to represent without prepossession the appearances of things; which delights in accidents, in unexpectedness, and sometimes, it must be confessed, in downright ugliness and awkwardness, it seems to me—what in short is sometimes called "impressionism," which has been largely influenced by Japanese art.

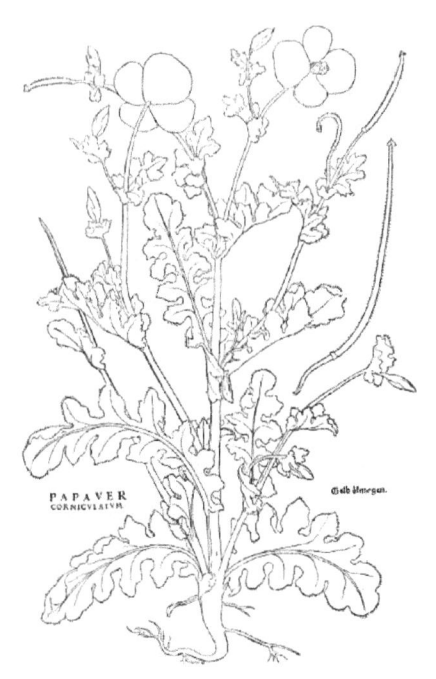

HORNED POPPY. FROM FUCHSIUS' "DE HISTORIA STIRPIUM," 1542.

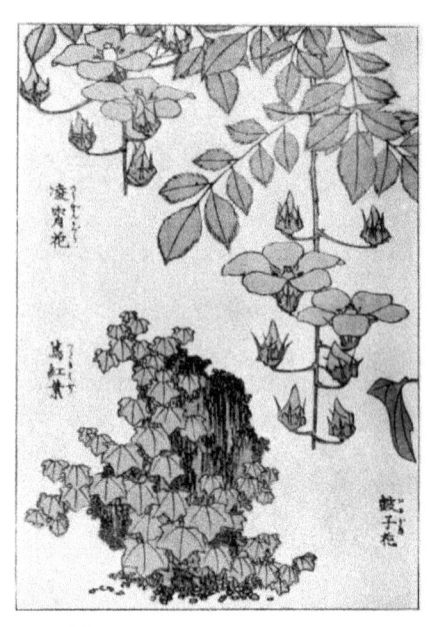

JAPANESE PLANT DRAWING. WOODCUT PRINTED IN COLOUR.

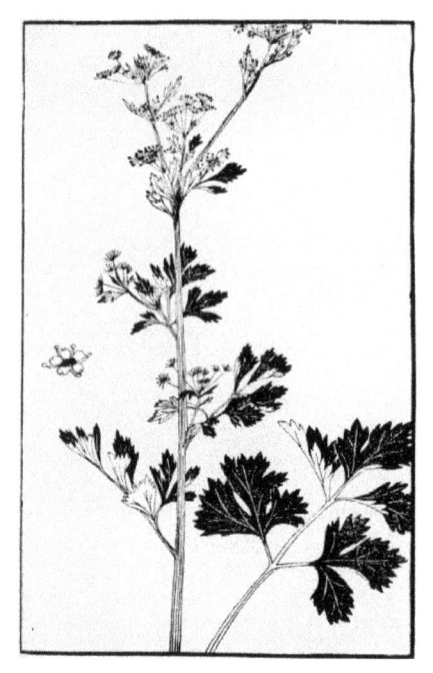

JAPANESE PLANT DRAWING. WOODCUT FROM A BOTANICAL WORK.

Mediæval brasses are often very fine in the quality and use of outline, and show a wonderful amount of exact characterization in portraiture, as well as beauty of ornamental effect in the use of plain surfaces relieved upon rich pattern work, and good disposition of draperies. Those of the fourteenth and fifteenth centuries, more especially the Belgian examples, are very useful to study for these things, as well as for the fine taste, the simplicity, and the broad artistic feeling shown under the strict limitation of the material, while they are remarkable for extraordinary delineation   of character by very simple means—the lines and sunk parts being incised in the smooth brass plate and filled in with black encaustic substance, while the colours of the heraldry are frequently enamelled. Note the beautiful lines of the drapery in the example given from Bruges, and the fine relief of the figures upon the rich diapered ground. In England the figures and borders were cut out in the brass and inserted in the stone slab, which formed the background; but the Flemish brasses show a different treatment, the figures being relieved upon a rich diapered ground, also incised upon the brass, which takes the form of a complete panel or plate covering the stone slab.

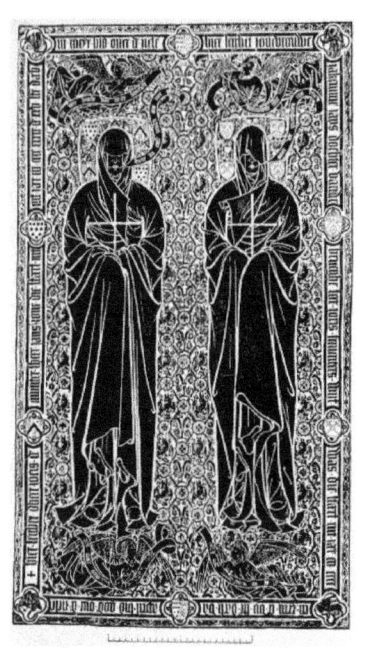

BRASS OF JORIS DE MUNTER AND WIFE (BRUGES, 1439). FROM CREENY'S "MONUMENTAL BRASSES."

One may trace in the later brasses the efforts of the designer to gain more relief and graphic emphasis in his figures by introducing lines of shading and cross lines and greater complexity generally, as well as a tendency to escape the limits of the panel, no doubt under the influence of the rising power of pictorial art, which from the Renascence onwards seems to have dominated by its influence all the other arts. But in the case of brasses the beauty of design, the charm and simplicity of the earlier treatment, as well as the rich decorative effect, disappear with the attempt to render complexities of effect and qualities of drawing for which the material and purpose were unsuited.

The same change of feeling left its mark upon the sculptor's work in sepulchral monuments and effigies, which, in the Gothic period up to the end of the fifteenth century, are frequently refined and beautiful pieces of delicate portraiture, wrought with extreme care and elaboration, with a strong yet restrained sense of the ornamental value of the detail; but which, under the pictorial influence and the search for more obvious and superficial naturalism, became more or less forced in effect and vulgarized in sentiment as well as execution, and finally lost in classical artificiality and theatric pomp.

KING ERIC MENVED AND QUEEN INGEBORG OF DENMARK (RINGSTEAD, 1319). FROM CREENY'S "MONUMENTAL BRASSES."

In simple draughtsmanship and purely graphic design, too, it is noticeable that, with the introduction of the copper-plate and the attempt to get in book illustrations something like pictorial values and chiaroscuro, how, by degrees, vigour of design and feeling for good line work was lost.

The revival of the woodcut even under Bewick did little to help line design—its former close companion. Bewick and his school developed the woodcut from the pictorial point of view, and with the object of demonstrating the capacity of the wood for rendering certain fine textures and tones as against steel and copper. Their great principle was the use of white line, not unheard of even in the early printing days, as a frontispiece to a German book ("Pomerium de Tempore," Augsburg, 1502) of the early sixteenth century testifies.

Bewick's birds, which are remarkable for the delicate, truthful way in which the plumage is rendered, are as much the work of a naturalist as of an artist, and they show but little design or feeling apart from this.

Although William Blake and Edward Calvert made notable use of the woodcut, it was not really until about the middle of the century that any serious attempt was made in the direction of the revival of line and pen drawing for the sake of its expressive vigour, ornamental possibilities, and autographic value. Probably it really began with German artists like Schnorr (who did a series of Bible pictures more or less after the manner of Holbein), Alfred Rethel, and Moritz Schwind. Rethel's two large woodcuts, "Death the Friend" and "Death the Enemy," are tolerably well known and show strong draughtsmanship and tragic force, recalling in their intensity and vigour the work of Dürer and the old German masters.

CHARLES KEENE. REDUCED FROM A HALF-PAGE DESIGN IN "PUNCH."

In England the revival of line design arose out of the Pre-Raphaelite movement (a movement certainly influenced by the study of early Italian as well as German and Flemish art), and was illustrated by the work of some of the leaders of that movement themselves.

The drawings (engraved on wood by the brothers Dalziel) by D. G. Rossetti, Holman Hunt, and Millais, which illustrate the edition of Tennyson's poems published in 1857, show perhaps the first definite experiments in this direction.

The pages of the journal "Once a Week," started in 1859, were the means of the introduction of new and powerful designers in line, such as Frederick Sandys, Charles Keene, E. J. Poynter, and Frederick Walker.

The first three showed unmistakable evidence of a study of the manner of German Renascence woodcuts, but it was allied to the matter of modern thought and naturalism. With a freer graphic naturalism of a different order, Walker united a certain grace and sentiment derived from classic sculpture, curiously mixed with a Dutch-like domestic feeling. In his black and white drawing he shows, too, I think, to some degree the influences of the photograph, which since those days has had so obvious an effect upon art and artists.

LINLEY SAMBOURNE. REDUCED FROM A FULL-PAGE DESIGN IN "PUNCH."

"Once a Week," which introduced these with other artists to the public, was started by the proprietors of "Punch," which had long maintained and still maintains an effective and legitimate field for graphic drawing in line rendered by the facsimile wood-block. The work of John Leech and Richard Doyle is well known, the former, with a light and somewhat loose touch registering the fashions and foibles of English life from week to week, with extraordinary spirit, humour, and character, often conveyed by very slight means.

Sir John Tenniel, with his more serious and heavier style, continued until recently to give his familiar allegories of the political situation; this style again has, I think, been influenced by German work.

Then Charles Keene brought in a kind of impressionistic naturalism, expressed by a method of his own, having a look of great freshness and directness, like crisp sketches from nature.

Du Maurier developed a different style, less vigorous but more graceful in drawing, and with certain leanings at one time to the romantic Pre-Raphaelitism he used his pencil occasionally to caricature.

In Mr. Linley Sambourne we see a designer and draughtsman of considerable power. His pen-line is vigorous and his drawing solid and graphic, with considerable feeling for style, but showing, I think, the influence of the photograph in the rendering of light and shade.

In quality of line there is a certain kinship with the work of Mr. Phil May, a later addition to the staff, though his treatment is very different. He represents, indeed, rather the modern impressionist feeling in line drawing influenced by the Japanese; his outlines are often extraordinarily graphic, and convey a great amount of character with very slight variation, and very little detail; but there is rather a noticeable tendency towards awkward composition and ugly or repulsive types.

PHIL MAY. FROM "PUNCH."

As a work giving some of the more serious and carefully studied designs in line and black and white of modern artists, engraved on wood, might be mentioned the Bible projected by the brothers Dalziel, a portion only of which was completed, consisting of a series of fine drawings by Holman Hunt, Madox Brown, E. J. Poynter, Frederic Leighton, and others. They are more perhaps in the nature of isolated pictures than book illustrations, but they are full of good and careful work.

The earlier etchings of Mr. Whistler are full of delicate drawing of the picturesque detail of old waterside houses, as in the famous "Wapping," which even survived translation into a process block in the "Daily Chronicle."

We have now a vast public apparently interested in, and accustomed to, graphic representation in black and white, through the continual multiplication of cheap illustrated newspapers, magazines, and books, and the continual invention and adaptation to the press of cheap photographic and automatic means of reproduction, which have almost entirely displaced the woodcut as a popular medium for the interpretation of graphic art.

In these cheap forms of pictorial art the photograph continues to gain ascendency not only as a medium for reproduction, but as a substitute for original artistic invention and design. Now while in the former province it is of enormous practical value, in the latter, I think, it bids fair to be extremely seductive and injurious to the growth of healthy artistic taste and capacity.

Modern painting and draughtsmanship have for a long time shown the influence of the photograph (which for certain illusory qualities of lighting and relief cannot be approached), and so, no doubt, artists themselves have prepared the way for its popularity, and perhaps even usurpation of the dominion of popular art.

So far, however, as photographic effect is preferred, and the mechanical tone-block is preferred to the pen-drawing and woodcut, it means the loss of character, of the personal element, of distinctive artistic style. It means, in short, the substitution of scientific invention and mechanical method for artistic imagination, observation, and variety—surely this would be a most unfortunate exchange.

CHAPTER IX.—OF THE INDIVIDUAL INFLUENCE IN DESIGN

WE commonly speak of ancient *art*, but of modern *artists*. Straws indicate which way the wind blows, and superficial habits may indicate changes of thought and feeling which lie far deeper. Interest has now become centred in the development of individual varieties rather than typical forms, whereas, as we have seen, it is the latter character that distinguishes the art of the ancients. In the great monumental works of the Asiatic nations of antiquity names of individual artists are lost, and in the art of Egypt and Assyria and Persia they are of little consequence, since certain prevailing types and methods were adhered to; and most of their work, as in their mural sculptures, while distinct in racial character, might almost have been executed by the same hand—Egyptian, Assyrian, or Persian, as the case may be. Tennyson's lines regarding nature might be here applied to art;

"So careful of the type she seems,
So careless of the single life."

With the intellectual activity of Greece and the development of her power as a state, the archaic and purely typical period in her arts, while possessing wonderful harmony and unity, led to individual development of artists, and, assisted no doubt by the increase of writing and record, famous names are handed down: such as Ictinus, the architect of the Parthenon, and Phidias, its sculptor, whose name characterizes the finest period of Greek art.

The ancient myth of Dædalus seems to show that art was always a power among the ancient Greeks, and Dædalus, who seems to occupy an analogous position in southern mythology to that of Wayland Smith in the north, may have represented, or his name and fame covered, whole generations of artists and cunning craftsmen; following the tendency, still noticeable, by which great reputations absorb smaller ones, and in the course of time have attributed to them works not really belonging to them at all. The name becomes a convenient symbol for a whole period, school, or group of workmen.

One can understand in primitive times how important the artist-craftsmen must have been: the fashioner of weapons, the one learned in the mysteries of smelting metal, of working iron, bronze, brass and copper, gold and silver, and having the power of making things of beauty out of these, which became the revered or coveted treasures of temples and kings' houses.

The old stories of the early Greek painters Apelles and Protogenes show, too, at once the tendency towards myth-making, and the old love of talk about art, as well as the old and dearly-clung-to popular theory that the beauty of painting is measured by its illusive power; so that the realistic grapes of Apelles, which only deceived the birds, were supposed to be outdone by the naturalistic curtain of Protogenes, which took in the critics. This tradition seems still to linger in the minds of our scene-painters when they present us with those wonderful (and sometimes fearful) drop curtains of satin, festooned with tassels and cords of undreamed-of sumptuousness and mysterious mechanism.

The names and works of Praxiteles and of Myron are well known to students of antique sculpture, and these are but stars of greater magnitude among a host of others less distinguished, or less centralized in universal fame. Yet we only know the Venus of Melos from the island where she was discovered.

We know that the Greek vase painters frequently signed their designs, and this has considerably helped the historic criticism and classification of that interesting and beautiful province of Greek design, such as has been so ably done in the works of Miss Jane E. Harrison.

In the Byzantine and early mediæval period we again see a great development of typical symbolical and profoundly impressive art in architecture and decoration, but again names and individual artists are largely lost. We do not know, for instance, who were the designers of the splendid mosaics at Ravenna.

With the dawn of painting in Italy, however, in the thirteenth century arose a personal and individualized type of art in which names became of immense interest. This was no doubt fostered by the rivalry of the cities, each independent, under its own government; each municipality proud and anxious to vie in the splendour and beauty of art with its neighbouring municipality. This led to a wholesome emulation among artists and very fine results, since there were abundant opportunities in the great public monuments, council chambers, and churches for the highest exercise of the architect, the painter, and craftsman's art.

The ancient system of the master craftsman working with his pupils in his shop or studio prevailed. A man might learn the craft of painting from the beginning, the grinding of colours, the laying of grounds, the mixing of tints, drawing out cartoons, enlarging designs for wall-painting, the painting of ornamental framework, and decorative detail, and gesso work enrichment, and gilding, miniature painting and the decoration of books, altar-pieces, signs and shrines; perhaps embroidery and textile patterns, banners, the furniture of shows and pageants—all these might be carried on, perhaps under one master. The term painter was not then specialized to mean either house-painter or easel-picture painter. An apprentice might thoroughly and practically learn his trade in the ordinary sense of the word, but it would depend upon his personal capacity and quality whether he would become a master, whether his name would be inscribed on the scroll of fame to be a landmark for future historians of art.

The romantic tales and episodes in the lives of painters which have come down to us are always interesting, and in Italy, being the centre of artistic life from the fourteenth to the end of the sixteenth centuries, we find abundant lore of this sort.

That picturesque legend of Cimabue of Florence, first told by Lorenzo Ghiberti (who was born in 1378), for instance, finding the youthful Giotto as a shepherd boy, while riding in the valley of Vespignano, about fourteen miles from Florence, sketching the image of one of his flock upon a smooth fragment of slate with a pointed stone, and taking him to Florence as his pupil.

Cimabue is commonly supposed to have been the first to show a new departure in the direction of greater freedom and naturalness of treatment, the first whose work shows much individuality, and emerges from the somewhat set and prescribed traditions of the Byzantine school which characterizes the earliest Italian painting of the Christian period really influenced by the Greek church mosaic design, which may be considered almost as the swathing clothes of mediæval painting in Italy.

His altar-piece for the church of Sta. Maria Novella was carried in procession through Florence to the church—a subject which has furnished a theme for Lord Leighton's well-known and fine decorative early work, too seldom seen.

Cimabue's portrait in the white embroidered costume with a hood, appears in a group with Giotto and other famous contemporaries, including Petrarch and Laura, in a fresco by Simone Memmi, a contemporary painter, on the wall of the chapel of the Cappella degli Spagnoli at Sta. Maria Novella.

But Giotto marks the real point of departure. Coming straight from outdoor life, from the simple country pursuits of a shepherd boy, it was significant that he should be the first to introduce a new spirit into art. Natural simplicity and directness, power of dramatic narrative painting, dignity and simplicity of style, and decorative beauty—these were some of the qualities with which Giotto enriched the field of early Italian art.

Alinari Photo.]

SIMONE MEMMI. FRESCO CONTAINING PORTRAITS OF CIMABUE, GIOTTO, AND CONTEMPORARIES. (FLORENCE. CLOISTERS OF S. M. NOVELLA.)

He became the friend of Dante, who pays him a tribute in the well-known lines in his poem "Il Purgatorio,"

"——— Cimabue thought
To lord it over painting's field; and now
The cry is Giotto, and his name's eclips'd."

CARY'S *Dante*.

And Giotto has left us an interesting portrait of the poet, on the wall of the Podesta, or council chamber of Florence, his first recorded work. Giotto was, in fact, a fellow pupil with Dante under the same master, Brunetto Latini, since Cimabue gave him all the cultivation of his time in books as well as art. The fame of Giotto as a painter spread all over Italy, and his services were required by the Church, and by rich and great persons.

There is a well-known story, which throws light upon his skill and certainty of hand, that once, when an emissary from Pope Boniface VIII. came to him for a specimen of his handiwork to show to his master, Giotto took a piece of paper and drew a circle in one stroke, without compasses.

The pope's emissary was disappointed at not getting a prettier picture, but it proved convincing,   and the legend passed into a proverb which runs: Rounder than the O of Giotto—"Più tondo che l' O di Giotto."

Alinari Photo.]

GIOTTO. PORTRAIT OF DANTE. (FLORENCE, PRETORIAN PALACE.)]

C. Naya Photo.]

GIOTTO. FRESCO (ARENA CHAPEL, PADUA).

C. Naya Photo.]

GIOTTO. FRESCO (ARENA CHAPEL, PADUA).

Alinari Photo.]

GIOTTO. "CHASTITY" (ASSISI).

Alinari Photo.]
GIOTTO. "OBEDIENCE" (ASSISI).

The frescoes of the Arena Chapel at Padua, representing the history of Christ and the Virgin in fifty square compartments, remain among Giotto's most famous works. The frescoes of the vaulted roof of the lower church at Assisi are also very fine.

"Here," says Mrs. Jameson, in "Early Italian Painters," "over the tomb of S. Francis, the painter represented the three vows of the order—Poverty, Chastity, and Obedience: and in the fourth compartment, the saint enthroned and glorified amidst the host of Heaven.

"The invention of the allegories under which Giotto has represented the vows of the saint—his marriage with Poverty—Chastity seated in her rocky fortress—and Obedience with the curb and yoke—is ascribed by tradition to Dante."

He was architect and sculptor as well as painter, and the design of the beautiful Campanile of the Duomo at Florence is due to him.

Cimabue and Giotto's contemporary, the sculptor Niccolo Pisano, was another distinguished artist of the early Italian revival. He is said to have been inspired by the study of antique sculpture. A certain sarcophagus (Phædra and Hippolytus) by its life and movement is supposed to have suggested the character which he sought in his work. The dramatic vitality which he infused into his figures was certainly extraordinary, as his famous pulpit at Pisa demonstrates. There was some danger of losing monumental dignity and repose, but it meant a return to nature and life after a long period of restraint and convention which had become dead.

Alinari Photo.]
NICCOLO PISANO. PULPIT (PISA BAPTISTERY).

The revival, therefore, was both salutary and necessary, though it is not unnatural that painters should have profited most by its effects, and that painting should have become the leading and popular art, because most immediate and familiar in its appeal and the width of its sympathy and range.

For vivid dramatic intensity of conception and earnestness of purpose the work of Orcagna stands out among the early painters of Florence. Andrea Orcagna was the son of a goldsmith of Florence. The goldsmiths of the fourteenth and fifteenth centuries were in general excellent designers, and not unfrequently became painters, as in the instances of Francia, Ghirlandajo, Verrocchio, Andrea del Sarto. It was in his father's workshop that Andrea Orcagna first learned his art. He was born before 1310, and he painted at the Campo Santo in 1332. His famous work was the fresco still to be seen on the wall of the Campo Santo at Pisa—"The Triumph of

Death." It presents us with certain contrasts of life and death, of pleasure and pain, of pomp and pride and poverty, the severe life of the holy man, the gay life of the pleasure seeker. There is a striking group of huntsmen reining in their horses at the sight of certain grim coffins containing great and pompous personages in various stages of decay. Grotesque fiends, too, are seen hustling wicked ones into a fiery pit. Thus does the early painter enforce the old moral. Thus does he paint the sharp contrasts of life and death, the short life and the merry one; the careless worldling and the rich and powerful finally levelled by death; while the higher spiritual life and the virtues of self-denial and sacrifice are suggested by the pious and primitive life of the monks.

Alinari Photo.]

ORCAGNA. "TRIUMPH OF DEATH." FRESCO (CAMPO SANTO, PISA).

Alinari Photo.]
BENOZZO GOZZOLI. DETAIL FROM FRESCO (RICCARDI CHAPEL, FLORENCE).

Alinari Photo.]
BENOZZO GOZZOLI. "JOURNEY OF THE MAGI." FRESCO (RICCARDI CHAPEL, FLORENCE).

Such subjects were favourites all through the Middle Ages, and it may be remembered that Petrarch about this time wrote his "Triumphs," one of which is named "The Triumph of Death."

Brogi Photo.]
BENOZZO GOZZOLI. DETAIL OF FRESCO (RICCARDI CHAPEL, FLORENCE).

Brogi Photo.]
BENOZZO GOZZOLI. DETAIL OF FRESCO (RICCARDI CHAPEL, FLORENCE).

A gentler spirit is seen in the art of Benozzo Gozzoli (born *circa* 1424), a pupil of Fra Angelico, full of a love for nature, of trees and flowers and animals, and of decorative beauty, a delight in beautiful walled cities, in ornate dresses, in fair fresh faces of youths and maidens. It is the joy of life without the shadow of death, as of the visions of a serene spirit that joins the hands of the old pagan life and the new Christian ideals and reconciles them in a world of beauty.

In the frescoes of the Riccardi Chapel at Florence, Benozzo pictures, with loving faithfulness, the Medici princes riding out to the hunt in splendid equipment, in a high upland and wooded country such as one may find around Florence. The subject was "The Adoration of the Magi," represented upon the side walls, "The Nativity" being painted over the altar. The procession of the kings with gifts is seen winding over the hills of the rich and varied landscape, interspersed with groups like the princes, in which Lorenzo the Magnificent appears, and portraits of the painter, his friends, and contemporaries.

The fresh youthful faces are full of the zest and pleasure of life. The horses curvet and prance in their proud trappings, and the hounds pursue the flying deer, as if for pleasant pastime.

He gives us those charming groups of kneeling angels also in the same chapel. Or he tells the story of the building of the tower of Babel, or of

Noah, at Pisa, or of St. Augustine, at San Gimignano, with the same serenity and delight in subsidiary incident and ornament.

Brogi Photo.]

SANDRO BOTTICELLI. DETAIL FROM "THE ADORATION OF THE MAGI" (FLORENCE, UFFIZI GALLERY).

Another very distinct individuality in painting, reflecting the spirit of his time halfway between mediæval feeling and the revived paganism and humanism of the classical Renascence, was Botticelli. He was a pupil of the painter-monk Fra Filippo Lippi, and worked at Florence about the middle of the fifteenth century. He was one of the painters summoned to Rome in 1471 by Pope Sixtus IV. to paint the walls of the Sistine Chapel. He is spoken of as "our friend Botticelli" in Leonardo da Vinci's treatise on painting; but until comparatively recently, as compared with more often sounded names in the trumpet of fame, the beauty of his work has been singularly neglected.

That now generally admired and most poetic and beautiful work, "An Allegory of Spring," in the Accademia at Florence, was, about five and twenty years ago, hung in an obscure position; but of late, and probably largely owing to English taste and criticism, it is now brought prominently forward and is constantly copied. The lady who is supposed to witness the masque stands in the centre in a grove of orange trees, the ground covered with flowers, among which is seen the *fleur-de-luce* of Florence; Zephyrus is clasping the earth, and from her mouth fall flowers; next to her Flora, or Spring, with a beautiful robe embroidered with flowers, bears roses in her lap and scatters them. Then there is a group of the "Three Graces" dancing, while Hermes, as the herald of Spring, leads the procession. The picture is supposed to have formed one of a set of four. The second panel called "Summer," and showing Venus rising in her shell from the sea, with a draped figure about to throw a robe over her as she reaches the grassy shore, is in the Uffizi Gallery. There is also a remarkable allegory, "Calumny," in the same gallery, while our own National Gallery contains a characteristic Madonna and Child with angels. Botticelli's Madonnas are always distinguished by a peculiar expression of wistful pathos and a feeling unlike those of any other painter. There is also a charming small Nativity with a ring of angels, besides the very splendid vision of heaven. Botticelli also made illustrations to Dante.

Alinari Photo.]

BOTTICELLI. "LA PRIMA VERA." AN ALLEGORY OF SPRING (FLORENCE ACADEMY).

A severer and more distinctly classically inspired genius, yet with a certain northern hardness, we find in Mantegna, who was born near Padua, in 1431. He came, it is said, of very poor and obscure parents, and, like his great predecessor Giotto, Mantegna was employed in keeping sheep. Little is known of his early life, but he is found later as one of the pupils of Francesco Squarcione, a painter of Padua, but more famous for his teaching, his school being at that time the most renowned in all Italy, his pupils numbering one hundred and thirty-seven. He was a great student of the antique, and travelled over Italy and Greece in search of remains of ancient art, obtaining casts or copies of such sculptures he could not purchase or remove, so that Mantegna had no doubt exceptional facilities for the study of classical sculpture, which had so marked an influence upon his design.

C. Naya Photo.]
MANTEGNA. FROM THE BRONZE MONUMENT IN THE CHURCH OF S. ANDREA AT MANTUA.

He seems, too, to have been an indefatigable worker, and drew with great diligence from the statues, busts, bas-reliefs, and architectural ornaments he found in the school of Squarcione. "At the age of seventeen Andrea painted his first great picture for the church of Santa Sofia in Padua (now lost), and at the age of nineteen assisted in painting the chapel of St. Christopher in the Eremitani—representing on the vault the four evangelists." He is said to have given to these sacred personages the air and attitude of Greek or Roman philosophers, the type in fact confirmed by Raphael and afterwards generally adopted by Renascence artists.

A curious change or blending of other elements and a different feeling in Mantegna's work, softening the somewhat cold and rigid classicism, seems to have been brought about by his association with the Venetian painter Jacopo Bellini, the father of the two greater Bellinis (Giovanni and Gentile), whose daughter Nicolosia he married about this time (1450). This marriage with the daughter of Squarcione's rival, as Bellini was considered, and Mantegna's friendship with him, seems to have offended Squarcione and caused an estrangement, and even the active enmity of his first master, and eventually led to his quitting Padua. He painted some frescoes at Verona, and was invited to Mantua by Ludovico Gonzaga, and finally he entered the service of that prince. He was invited to Rome by Pope Innocent VIII. to paint a chapel in the Belvedere of the Vatican, which was actually destroyed in the last century by Pius VI. to make room for his new museum. This was after the ruthless way of the popes, prodigal of painted walls, as when the beautiful early Renascence frescoes of Melozzo da Forli were removed to make room for Raphael's and Giulio Romano's frescoes in the Stanzi.

There is a story of the discretion of Mantegna, which, with a natural courtesy, seems to have distinguished him personally. While working for Pope Innocent VIII. it happened that the payments for the work were not made with desirable regularity; the pope, visiting the artist at his work one day, asked him the meaning of a certain female figure which he had introduced. Andrea replied that he was trying to represent *Ingratitude*. The pope, understanding him at once, replied: "If you would place *Ingratitude* in fitting company, you should place Patience at her side." Andrea took the hint and said no more. It is satisfactory to know that in the end the pope not only paid up, but was "munificent" besides.

Finally, Mantegna returned to Mantua, where he built himself a magnificent house painted inside and out by his own hand, and in which he lived in great esteem and honour until his death in 1506. He was buried in the church of his patron St. Andrew, where his monument in bronze and several of his pictures are still to be seen.

The famous frieze of "The Triumph of Julius Cæsar"—which is now in Hampton Court Palace, having been bought by King Charles I. from the Duke of Mantua—was first designed by Mantegna for the hall of the palace of San Sebastiano at Mantua, and commenced in 1488, before he went to Rome, he finishing it after his return in 1492. There are nine panels or compartments in this frieze: "They are painted in distemper on twilled linen, which has been stretched on frames, and originally placed against the wall with arabesque pilasters dividing the compartments."

Mr. Alfred Marks issued a set of photographs some years ago, but they are not very clear, There is a good set of Italian woodcuts in chiaroscuro of the designs, by Andrea Andreani, done while the frieze was in the palace at

Mantua, which have been engraved in various ways at different times with very various results.

The whole design is extremely rich and sumptuous, and full of the extraordinary designing power and command of inventive detail so characteristic of Mantegna.

"In the first compartment we have the opening of the procession: trumpets, incense burning, standards borne aloft by the victorious soldiers.

"In the second, the statues of the gods carried off from the temples of the enemy; battering rams, implements of war, heaps of glittering armour carried on men's shoulders, or borne aloft in chariots.

"In the third compartment, more splendid trophies of a similar kind; huge vases filled with gold coin, tripods, etc.

"In the fourth, more such trophies, with the oxen crowned with garlands for the sacrifice.

"In the fifth are four elephants adorned with rich garlands of fruits and flowers, bearing on their backs magnificent candelabra, and attended by beautiful youths.

"In the sixth are figures bearing vases, and others displaying the arms of the vanquished.

"The seventh shows us the unhappy captives, who, according to the barbarous Roman custom, were exhibited on these occasions to the scoffing and exulting populace. There is here a group of female captives of all ages, among them a dejected bride-like figure, a woman carrying her infant children, and a mother her little boy, who lifts up his foot as if he had hurt it.

"In the eighth we have a group of singers and musicians.

ANDREA MANTEGNA. PART OF "THE TRIUMPH OF JULIUS CÆSAR" (FROM THE WOODCUT BY ANDREA ANDREANI).

"In the ninth, and last, appears the Conqueror, Julius Cæsar, in a sumptuous chariot richly adorned with sculptures; he is surrounded by a crowd of figures, and among them is seen a youth bearing aloft a standard on which is inscribed the boastful words: 'Veni, vidi, vici'—'I came, I saw, I conquered.'"[12]

The care and science of the draughtsmanship is as noticeable as the richness of the design. The perspective being carefully given as of figures actually seen above the eye-line, and with all the sumptuousness and the mixed elements of the design there is a certain restraint and monumental severity which preserves its dignity.

Rubens, when at Mantua in 1606, was struck by the splendour of the work, and gave a Rubensesque rendering of one of the compartments, which is in the National Gallery; but it loses the peculiar dignity, serenity, and decorative character of Mantegna's work in the somewhat florid and bumptious style of the late Flemish master; but there is no doubt that Rubens entertained a real admiration for the work, and was instrumental in getting Charles I. to purchase it.

Among Mantegna's chief works may be named "La Madonna della Vittoria," now in the Louvre, painted as an altar-piece for the church built by the Marquis of Mantua, to commemorate his victory on the retreat of

Charles VIII. from Italy; the Crucifixion, also in the Louvre, containing the artist's own portrait in the half-length figure of the soldier seen in front; the fine allegory of the Vices flying before Wisdom, Chastity, and Philosophy; and the beautiful Parnassus, which were painted for Isabella d'Este, and filled panels in a room in her palace at Mantua, as has recently been discovered. Mr. Armstrong has had a fine large scale model of one side of this room set up in the South Kensington Museum, to show the effect of the decorations complete of Mantegna's allegories (represented by copies). One must not forget either the wonderful Circumcision, at Florence, or, in our own National Gallery, the Virgin and Child enthroned.

Besides his paintings there exists a multitude of drawings, designs, and plates of his own engraving (an art which he took up when he was sixty years old). These include the fifth, sixth, and seventh compartments of his own "Triumph of Julius Cæsar."

Perhaps the greatest individual mind of the Italian Renascence was Leonardo da Vinci, who was so distinguished in so many different departments of thought and art; and while he summed up and passed beyond the philosophical and scientific knowledge of his age, and experimented in nearly all directions, and was at once architect, chemist, engineer, musician, poet, his fame still rests upon his achievements in painting, which are distinguished by a peculiar refinement, extreme finish, and intellectual and poetic quality. He was born at Vinci, from which he takes his name, near Florence—that Athens of the Middle Ages—in the lower Val d'Arno, on the borders of the territory of Pistoia. His father was an advocate, not rich, but able to give his son the advantage of the best instructors in the science and art of that period. He studied under Andrea Verrocchio (famous for his superb bronze equestrian statue of the Coleoni at Venice), himself uniting the arts of sculptor, chaser in metal, and painter. There is a story that Leonardo as a youth was set to paint an angel in a picture of Verrocchio, and so outdid his master that the latter never touched painting again.

A weird fantastic vein which appears in Leonardo's work, especially in his love for inventing grotesques, comes out in the tale of the fig tree. A peasant on his father's estate cut down an old fig tree and brought a section of the trunk to have something painted upon it for his cottage. Leonardo determined to do something terrible and striking—a beautiful horror which should rival the mythical Medusa's head (which he afterwards painted), and, aided by his natural history studies and the reptiles he collected, he produced a sort of monster or chimera which frightened his father into fits and was therefore considered too good for the peasant's cottage, and afterwards sold for much. The peasant was persuaded to give up his fig tree and put off with a wooden shield painted with a device of a hart transfixed with an arrow.

In a letter to the Duke of Milan, who had invited him to his court, he thus recites his qualifications as an artist: "I understand the different modes of sculpture in marble, bronze, and terra-cotta. In painting, also, I may esteem myself equal to anyone, let him be who he may."

Of his paintings the widest-known, through engravings, is "The Last Supper," which was painted on the wall of the refectory of the Dominican Convent of the Madonna delle Grazie at Milan, occupying two years, from 1496 to 1498—but the fresco has suffered by time and restoration, and but little of it is now left. There is a fine study of the head of Christ.

Brogi Photo.]

LEONARDO DA VINCI. FRESCO OF "THE LAST SUPPER."

The picture of the Virgin of the Rocks and the portrait, Madonna Lisa del Gioconde, in the Louvre, show the quality of his painting—the characteristic subtlety of expression, mysteriousness, and very elaborate finish.

After his return to Florence began his rivalry with another gigantic artistic personality of that time of wonders—Michael Angelo, who was then, in the early years of the sixteenth century, about twenty-two years younger. The strong but jealous individuality of both, in spite of admiration for each other's genius, unfortunately stood in the way of friendship and co-operation. They remained rivals and competitors. They contended for the painting of the great Council Hall in the Palazzo Vecchio at Florence, and both prepared cartoons. Leonardo chose for his subject the defeat of the Milanese by the Florentine army in 1440; Michael Angelo a party of Florentine soldiers surprised while bathing in the Arno. Leonardo's design was chosen, but he spent so much time in experimenting and in preparing the wall to receive oil-painting, which he preferred to fresco, that, changes of government happening, the scheme was finally abandoned, and both cartoons, though shown for several years, were finally lost, only a copy of Michael Angelo's remaining, and an engraving from it.

The experimental nature of Leonardo seems to have prevented his completing many works, while he was full of projects of all kinds, too many of which were never realized. The fine cartoon of the Virgin and St. Anna was never painted. This cartoon, or a good copy, is now in the possession of the Royal Academy.

Alinari Photo.]

LEONARDO DA VINCI. STUDY FOR THE HEAD OF CHRIST.

In 1514 Leonardo was, like so many great Italian artists, invited to Rome by the pope (then Leo X.), but more in his character of philosopher, mechanic, and alchemist than as a painter. There he met Raphael, then at the height of his fame, engaged in painting the Stanzi of the Vatican. But Leonardo was ill-pleased on the whole with his Roman visit. The pope was said to have become dissatisfied with his speculative and dilatory habits. His old rival, Michael Angelo, was there, and finally he left and set out for Pavia, where Francis I. of France then held his Court. By him Leonardo was received with honour and favour, and went with him to France as principal Court painter, only, however, as it proved, to die there on May 2nd, 1516.

In the work of Leonardo's great rival, Michael Angelo, the art of the Italian Renascence may be said to have reached its culminating point, and after him decline sets in. It is as if the wonderful structure of inventive artistic genius had been piled by the life labours of generations to an ambitious and dangerous height, and at last had given way under the strain, or perhaps, like the sun-flower, the same force which raises the splendid rayed head and enables it to outface the sun, at last forces it earthwards again.

Michael Angelo Buonarotti was born at Settignano, near Florence, in the year 1474. His ambition, personal pride, and masterfulness of temper possibly may be traced to his progenitors—a once noble family. It was, too, against the prejudice of his father that he finally decided his career, becoming the apprentice of Ghirlandajo, It was in the days when Lorenzo the Magnificent ruled over Florence, and the young Michael Angelo became a student in the Academy, founded upon the strength of a collection of antique marbles, busts, statues, fragments in the palace and gardens of that prince. This alone would be sufficient to give a strong classical bias to his style.

Alinari Photo.]
BUST OF MICHAEL ANGELO BUONAROTTI (S. CROCE, FLORENCE).

There is a story of Michael Angelo's first attempt in marble when he was about fifteen—a copy of an antique mask of an old laughing faun: he treated this with a spirit and vivacity of his own, and Lorenzo de Medici was struck by its cleverness; but he said, "Thou shouldst have remembered that old folks do not retain all their teeth: some of them are always wanting." The young sculptor at once struck one or two out, giving the mask a more grotesque expression.

On this evidence of cleverness Lorenzo took entire charge of Michael Angelo. With the marks of princely favour, however, he was destined to carry another mark, not so agreeable, ever after, owing to, as some say, the jealousy of Torregiano, a fellow pupil, who in a quarrel struck him, some accounts say with his fist, some with a mallet, and so gave him the broken nose which is characteristic of the portraits of Michael Angelo. Torregiano in consequence suffered banishment from Florence. In his own account of the affray to Benvenuto Cellini he declares the provocation came from Michael Angelo. The favour and protection of Lorenzo did not last long, as in his eighteenth year Michael Angelo lost his patron by death.

It was Lorenzo's son Piero who set him one wintry day to make a statue out of the snow—rather a wasteful proceeding for a Michael Angelo, though, as the late Mr. Walter Pater has said, there is a certain reminiscence of the feeling of the snow statue in the suggestive and half-finished figures of the tombs of the Medici.

A. Braun & Co. Photo.]

MICHAEL ANGELO. "THE CREATION OF MAN" (CEILING, SISTINE CHAPEL).

With the fall of the Medici family and their exile from Florence, Michael Angelo, as one of their retainers, had to fly also, and took refuge in Bologna, where he pursued his work as a sculptor. At the age of twenty-two he produced the "Pietà" in marble, now in St. Peter's at Rome.

In 1502 he was again recalled to Florence. In 1504 took place the competition with Leonardo of the cartoons for the Palazzo Vecchio, already spoken of.

In 1506 Michael Angelo was called to Rome by Pope Julius II. The pope employed him to design the sumptuous sculptural monument destined for his own tomb, for which the famous colossal Moses was executed, and the slaves or prisoners, but these, like the tomb, never were finished.

But his great work in Rome, the great work of his life, was the decoration of the ceiling of the Sistine Chapel, the walls of which had been painted by earlier artists of the Florentine school: Signorelli, Cosimo Rosselli, Perugino, Ghirlandajo, Botticelli. The ceiling remained unadorned, and now Michael Angelo was called upon to design his great sacred epic of painting, having to deal with a space 150 feet in length by 50 feet in breadth, upon the concave surface of a round vault, without any architectural or structural enrichment or division save the windows. The theme was the fall and redemption of mankind according to the Bible history.

MICHAEL ANGELO. CEILING OF THE SISTINE CHAPEL.

At first it appears that Michael Angelo, as it is said, doubtful of his own skill in fresco, called in the aid of painters from Florence to aid him in carrying out his design, but was so disappointed with their work that he effaced it and dismissed them. He then shut himself up and proceeded to devote himself to the gigantic work alone, preparing the colours with his own hands, showing how thorough an individualist he must have been, contrary to the practice of his own time, which was to work with pupils and assistants. He began with the end towards the door, and in two compartments first painted "The Deluge" and "The Vineyard of Noah"; the figures are on a smaller scale, which he afterwards abandoned for a larger, bolder treatment. He spent twenty-two months in painting the ceiling, exclusive of the time spent in preparing the cartoons. The work was uncovered to the public view on All Saints' Day, 1512.

The sculpturesque and architectural feeling which, really stronger in Michael Angelo's work than that of the painter, is very decidedly manifested both in the general plan of the design and in individual figures and details. In order to bring so great a scheme into comprehensive form it was necessary to divide and subdivide the blank ceiling with painted architectural mouldings and ribs into spaces and panels. The titanic youthful figures placed between, upon the ledges and brackets of the framework of the subjects, are very fine and characteristic in style, and essentially sculptors' designs; each would work out as a separate statue, though for all that each single figure, as each figure of every group, bears a certain relation to the rest and fills a harmonious and necessary place in the scheme. The colour is subdued and quiet. It has a gray, cool effect in the chapel, gray blues, pale greens and whites being much used in the draperies, and the chief decorative effect being gained by the opposition of brown flesh tones to the broad, light marble-like framework, or the landscape and sky backgrounds of the subject panels. This great work was completed by Michael Angelo in his thirty-ninth year.

Alinari Photo.]

MICHAEL ANGELO. "THE DELPHIC SIBYL" (SISTINE CHAPEL).

Alinari Photo.]

MICHAEL ANGELO. TOMB OF GIULIANO DE MEDICI. FLORENCE.

Alinari Photo.]

MICHAEL ANGELO. TOMB OF LORENZO DE MEDICI. FLORENCE.

Another great monumental work in which his architectural and sculptural genius come out are the tombs of the Medici in the Church of San Lorenzo. The seated figures of Lorenzo and Giuliano de Medici are placed in the recesses of a Renascence arcade, in front of which are marble sarcophagi, and upon the lids recline figures of Night and Morning, and of Dawn and Twilight respectively. They are very bold and powerful in design, and extremely characteristic in style and treatment, having a certain titanic energy and tragic unrest, as well as pensive mystery, about them, which belong to the strong personality of their designer.

Poet, as well as painter, architect, and sculptor, we see him moving amid the political troubles and vicissitudes of his time, a proud and stormy spirit, a man of extraordinary energy, which impresses itself upon all his works. The designer of St. Peter's, the painter of the Sistine, and anon as engineer called to fortify Florence; austere and abstemious of habit, proud and imperious, and yet tenderly solicitous for his aged father, and devoted to his old servant Urbino, whom he tenderly nursed in his last illness.

The great artist lived till eighty-nine, and died in Rome, the scene of his monumental labours, on February 18th, 1564.

As showing the alertness and activity of his mind in old age, he is said to have made a drawing of himself as an aged man in a go-cart, with the motto, *Ancora impara* (still learning), a true emblem for a great man who, in spite of his knowledge, feels that in view of the unknown he knows nothing.

These are a few, a very few, individualities out of the drama of Italian art, briefly sketched, but distinct as they are, they are not detached like isolated statues upon pedestals from the characteristics of their age. They are great because they embody those characteristics; they are like rich jewels strung upon a golden chain—the golden chain of inventive tradition which unites them—which, while leaving each artist free in his own sphere, brings his work into relation and harmony with that of his contemporaries, his predecessors, and his successors. Some may prefer to take the jewels separately and admire them without reference to the chain; but, I think, to fully understand and appreciate the genius of individual artists one must never leave out of account their relation to their time, and its influences, the relation of their particular art to the state of the arts generally; for among these are the factors which have contributed to make them what we find them in their works; just as the colour and relief of a figure or a head depends largely upon its background.

CHAPTER X.—OF THE COLLECTIVE INFLUENCE

IN my last chapter I compared tradition in art to a golden chain, and the striking individualities which arise from time to time as the jewels upon such a chain. The history of art and the evolution of design may be regarded either from the point of view of the jewels or from the point of view of the ordinary links; and if we wish to take a just and comprehensive view I think we must not only consider the luminous points, but the system—the links—by which they are connected and related. Looking out into the clear night we see a vast mass of brilliant stars of all degrees of magnitude apparently flung into space without order or relation, but the studies of astronomers have revealed that they are the central suns of systems around which revolve planets invisible to us; but these star-suns themselves become lost, and merged in the countless myriads that form the silvery cloud we call the milky way. So it is in the history of art and the evolution of design. At first we are attracted by the brilliant personalities, surrounded by satellites, that seem to sum up in their work whole epochs, and remain typical and central points in the wide spaces of time; but further research reveals their relation to other personalities not so distinct, on whom the full light of popular favour has not flashed, and presently we get beyond personalities altogether, and in the work of remote antiquity see only the results of the labours of generations, purely typical forms of art, the monumental record of races, of nations, of dynasties, the work, not of individual men, but of collective *man*.

Of such we may find examples in the art of ancient Egypt, of Assyria, of Persia, and in the archaic and primitive art of all kinds, from the fragments of pottery from the plain of Troy to the carved paddles of the Polynesian islanders.

The art and craft of building—architecture, the fundamental art, can only be traced back to its primitive forms in different countries as practised among different races and peoples. The origin of its distinctive styles, and its principal constructive features, were determined long ago under the influence of climate and local materials, by the collective thought and co-operative labour of mankind schooled by necessity and experience.

Yes, it is a history of constant adaptation to conditions and united labour and invention from our primitive ancestor, who improved upon the natural shelter of the tree by interlacing its pendent branches with other branches and stakes fixed in the ground; who burned the ends of their timbers, so that as piles they could be driven more easily into the mud to support the platforms of the wattled lake dwellings, when there were no steel axes. From the early colonists of our race, the Aryan wagoners, who perhaps took the idea of the primitive gable and roof timbers from the tilt of the wagon, or the supports of the tent-coverings; from the ingenuity of the Mongolian settlers by the riverside, making the framing of their houses and supporting their roofs by the bamboo, utilizing the hollow canes for the jointing and bracketing of the supports, and terminating the ends ornamentally by inserting grotesquely carved heads. The chain of invention is unbroken up to modern scientific engineering and calculated principles of building construction, which but sums up and systematizes the collective experience of ages.

We see, too, the collective hand of tradition and the adherence to accustomed forms in the adoption or imitation of features of timber construction in stone construction and ornament by the ancients; as, for instance, in the form of the Persian capital from Persepolis, and in the dentil ornament of classical architecture mentioned in the preceding chapters.

Out of necessity springs construction; out of construction springs ornament. We cannot find the individual in either, both being the result of slow and gradual evolution, requiring long periods of time and continuity of custom, life, and habit, and the continuous associated labour of communities, wherein the individual is of less importance than the maintenance of the social organism. At first the preservation of the gens, the tribe, the protection and service of the village community, the handing on of tradition and folk-lore, until, with conquest and extension and consolidation into a nation, settled industries, and religious faith and ritual, the desire arises to clothe the mythical and spiritual ideas of a people in permanent monumental form and colour.

A cathedral represents the collective art, work, and thought of centuries. The names of its builders, its masons, its carvers, its glaziers, are lost; the heads and hands that carried out the work, whose invention and feeling, whose very life have been wrought into the stone and the wood and the glass, have left no other record. An abbot's or a bishop's name may be given as having planned or raised the money for this choir or that porch at different times, but the artists and craftsmen who did the work generally remain unknown. They worked in their craft in harmony with the workers in kindred crafts, and as brother members of their guild, and instead of building up merely personal reputations really evolved collectively the distinctive architectural style and decorative types of their age.

This is one reason why a Gothic cathedral is so impressive. We see the growth of an organic style, starting, perhaps, with the round arch and massive Norman pier, and passing through the transition to the lancet arch of the early pointed to the moulded arch and the clustered shaft and foliated capital, with the ribbed, vaulted roof covering the long nave with a network of recurring constructive lines, and meeting overhead in carved bosses, or spreading into Tudor fans. Or we may mark the gradual evolution of the window from the round headed, deep-set loop-hole of the Byzantine and Norman period into the long lancet-pointed panel of geometric glass; and see then how by degrees the light, first divided into two by a shaft, suggested the clustering of many lights together, as in great western or eastern windows, dividing them by mullions breaking into geometric tracery in the pointed heads; and thus raising a beautiful pierced screen of stone to hold the coloured glass and reveal its splendour against the full light of the sky.

Can we name the inventors of these changes, the evolvers of these beauties of our constructive art? Do we not feel that by their very nature they could not have been claimed by any individual mind alone or have reached perfection in a single lifetime? They are the natural result of a free and vital condition in art, moved by the unity of faith and feeling, wherein men work together as brothers in unity, each free in his own sphere, but never isolated, and never losing his sense of relation to the rest.

Thus we get the harmonious effect of a great orchestra, where, though every variety of instrument may be played, all are subordinated, or co-ordinated, to the musical scheme, and produce that impression of power and sweetness by cadences that may be now soft as the whispers of the summer winds over a field of wheat, and anon sweep like a tempest with the fury of thundering waves upon the utmost shores of sound.

The emotions produced by such forms of collective art lift the mind out of the personal region altogether; they are akin, indeed, to the feelings awakened in the presence of wild nature. We seem to hear the voice of Time himself out of the caverns of the past, the song of life, like that of a child in the sunlight, and the half-articulate, pathetic murmur of the voices of birds and beasts; the hush of the wood at noon-tide, the transfiguration of the afterglow, and the mystery of night.

In the primitive ornament of all peoples we find the same or similar typical forms constantly recurring, the germs of pattern design afterwards developed, complicated, and refined upon: the chequer, the zigzag, the fret, the circle, the spiral volute, the twisting scroll—can we ascribe their invention to any individual mind or hand? Can the mechanician tell us who were the inventors of the wheel, the lever, the mode of producing fire, the canoe, the paddle, the spade, the plough, the vessel of clay, the axe, the hammer, the needle, or even spinning and weaving? Yet they are inventions of incalculable importance to human life, which without them could not maintain itself, much less build upon them, as it were, the vast and complex structure of modern invention, of science, and of art.

A form in ornament once found, however, is repeated. The eye grows accustomed to it, takes delight in it, and expects its recurrence. It becomes established by use and wont, and is often associated with fundamental ideas of life and the universe itself. Thus we get traditional ornament, handed on from generation to generation, its origin and meaning perhaps lost—like the pictorial significance of the individual letters of our alphabet, which everybody uses, but which require a special kind of study and research to explain their real meaning and original forms.

Side by side with this liking for the accustomed, this demand for the expected, appears to have grown up another feeling, a love of change and variety equally natural and human.

NATURAL VARIATION IN REPETITION OF ORNAMENTAL FORMS. PRIMARY SCHOOL CHILDREN DRAWING ON THE BLACKBOARD, PHILADELPHIA.

NATURAL VARIATION IN REPETITION OF ORNAMENTAL FORMS. PRIMARY SCHOOL CHILDREN DRAWING ON THE BLACKBOARD, PHILADELPHIA.

In ornament variation may at first be unconscious, and might have arisen from the natural tendency of the hand to vary a form in repeating it (as our own experience will tell us), while it requires an effort to reproduce its exact counterpart. This tendency to vary the same form, in repeating it, by different individuals is illustrated by the little American children cultivating their facility of hand by drawing on the blackboard. This natural variation, having a rich and pleasant effect, is encouraged until conscious and studied invention and ingenuity of individual artists in the varying of designs take its place.

Tradition in design may no doubt be largely attributed to the influence of the workshop, or what we should now call technical necessities, the use of certain tools and materials giving a certain character of their own in the rendering of form, as one may see even in the case of such a matter as quality of outline (important enough in all design) if we compare the differences between a form drawn with the pencil, the pen, with the brush, or with charcoal. A certain typical treatment becomes naturally evolved in the course of practice which seems proper to each method, while the treatment is sure to be slightly varied in the hands of every individual. Of course a strong artistic personality may greatly modify tradition in any art, though such an one is seldom entirely free from its influence; and the greatest artists in past times have generally built upon it, and have become what they are rather because of an existing vital tradition admitting of individual variation.

This was largely the case, I think, with the great masters of the Italian Renascence, some of whom I spoke of in the previous chapter. The general standard of excellence was maintained by their contemporaries. A great individual artist arises and only by degrees distinguishes himself by his personal choice and treatment, his variation of practice or method, grafting on to the stem perhaps some new rare flower. He raises the standard higher, he imports new elements, he influences tradition, and the lamp is handed on.

Giotto's art would not have been what it was but for the Byzantine influence under which he was trained. Without losing certain fine qualities of the dignity and serenity of the earlier art, he infused fresh life and prepared the way for the greater freedom and naturalism of his successors. The various schools of painting are closely linked, and if the links were complete we should perhaps be more struck with the resemblances, the similarities, than the differences.

The great structure of style is raised stone by stone: the labour of generations of artists gradually advances the standard of excellence. Now and then a greater mind appears, and by some new thought or method, fresh sentiment or point of view, raises the standard higher, and so an epoch is marked in art.

Great cleavages from time to time occur which disturb the orderly progression and connection, like cataclysms in nature—earthquakes and upheavals which break the continuity of the geologic beds and throw them upon different levels; but the strong social and collective tendency in man is always to repair and reform, to re-unite scattered fragments and to form new traditions both in life and art.

In an age which has seen the development of an organized industrial system of extraordinary and minute division of labour under the factory system, and has now entered an epoch of further specialization of labour with the invention and use of complicated machinery driven by steam and electric power, in association with which labour becomes not only specialized but almost automatic, we perhaps hardly need reminding of the collective influence, since for the effective supply of the big world-market *all* products are the result of collective human labour.

Such an organization of machine production as every effective factory displays, of collective labour, though not organized for the collective benefit, but rather wastefully contending with other factories for private profit-making in a fierce and unscrupulous warfare of commercial competition—such organizations can hardly be favourable to the production of fine and beautiful art. The art, the wonder, the invention, if anywhere, must really be sought in the means rather than the ends. The machines which produce our wares are marvels of ingenuity, of mechanical adaptation, of economy of force, but the finished product is often most depressing. One may see in print works, for instance, those wonderful colour printing machines capable of printing seven, and even twelve, colours from the rollers in succession upon the cloth as it passes through, often turning out extremely tame and commonplace patterns on cheap material, which look much more interesting as engraved upon the polished copper roller than they ever do on the cloth.

Well, it may be said, the remedy is with us—with the designers. We have only to use our invention in producing good and attractive designs, adapted to the process and material, and the factory and the machine will do the rest.

AXMINSTER CARPET WEAVING.

It is conceivable, certainly, that where the object is *solely* to produce something at once beautiful and serviceable, by a chain of associated and intelligent labour, with the most ingenious machines at the command of the designers, wonderful things might be done; but it is a question whether, if a design be ever so good, we should not grow tired of it if we saw it produced in enormous quantities. Yet *that*, after all, is the object of our factories, of our improved machinery, to produce in enormous quantities—not primarily to supply the world's needs either, but in order to sell at a profit. Art, however, is only concerned with quality—to make everything as good of its kind as possible, to seek variety, beauty, appropriateness.

TAPESTRY CARPET WEAVING.

We have yet to see whether industrial production, organized on the modern system, is equal to the old handicraftsman with his simple methods, as far as artistic results are concerned.

So far the Indian, with his hand-block printing his pattern on his strip of muslin or cotton, or dipping his tied cloth into the dye, produces more artistic results than all our wonderful machinery. Mechanical perfection is one thing, and artistic feeling quite another, and the more as an end a people seeks after the first the less it is likely to care for or understand the other.

The chain of production, too, may be mechanically complete, as in our best factories it may be said to be as far as organization goes, yet we may be still far from the finer sympathetic chain of *artistic* association by means of which the best work is produced. In this we must include the stimulus of external beauty and harmonious surroundings, as well as individual freedom.

Such a condition of things might have been found in any craft's-guild, and seen in full working order in any workshop of the Middle Ages.

Such an interior as is pictured by Etienne Delaune, a celebrated goldsmith of Paris, as late as the sixteenth century, of his own atelier, engraved by himself, shows us a group of artist craftsmen working together with all the tools and implements of their art around them. Of the three seated at the bench one is engraving or chasing; another at work upon a watch, drilling apparently; while the third is doing some fine *repoussé* work. The young man at the furnace is probably enamelling, and a boy at the wheel appears to be wire-drawing. A great variety of tools are placed in exemplary order upon the walls—pincers, pliers, files, shears, hammers, punches, a small anvil, crucibles, and a pair of bellows for the furnace.

INTERIOR OF THE ATELIER OF ETIENNE DELAUNE, PARIS, 1576.

There are still some crafts which are worked in this simple artistic co-operative way, and have undergone but little changes of method since the Middle Ages. Indeed, one might say *all* the finer artistic handicrafts; and it is noteworthy that the tools used are of the same type—the sculptor's mallet and chisel, the painter's palette and brushes, for instance, have remained practically unchanged in form from time immemorial.

Those who have seen glass blowing and the formation of glass vessels must have been struck by the skill and celerity displayed by the craftsmen at the furnace mouth, under very trying conditions, and also by the necessity of effective help at certain movements, when the molten glass is made to revolve upon the bar by one man, while the shape is given to it by another. The master craftsman generally seems to have two assistants, but the amount of co-operation necessary in forming the vessels depends much upon their size, small pieces being completed by one alone.

There are glass works still working, such as those at Whitefriars, which have been there since the sixteenth century. The circle of furnace mouths, the ruddy glow falling upon the faces and figures of the workers, form a striking scene. By a skill of manipulation that might well appear magical seen for the first time, the craftsmen produce vessels of any variety of shape, constantly returning the work as it progresses to the fire. Though the work seems to lend itself to the varying invention of the designer, they can reproduce the section sketched in chalk on a black panel at the side of the furnace in a completed form to exact measurement.

GLASS BLOWING.

The art of the printer of books, to which so much interest has of late been drawn, and which has been revived as an art by Mr. William Morris at his Kelmscott Press, affords another instance of the necessity of intelligent and artistic co-operation.

INTERIOR OF A PRINTING OFFICE IN THE SIXTEENTH CENTURY (FROM JOST AMMAN).

To begin with, there is the paper; a good tough handmade paper, like drawing paper, is wanted for rich and bright impressions of type or woodcuts. This must be made from the best linen rags, and each sheet is manipulated by the hands, by means of a wired frame of wood dipped into the pulp and cunningly shaken so that it (the pulp) shall spread over the wires evenly to form, when dry, the sheet of paper.

Then the type-founding must be looked after. Lettering of good form must be designed, and so designed that each letter must be separate and yet capable of forming words without undue gaps, and also legible pages of agreeable type, good in the mass and good in the single letters and words. The type-founder and designer must therefore be a man of taste and cultivation, he must have a knowledge of alphabets, of early printing and of historic MSS. and calligraphy, and he must be a capable designer, able to appreciate the niceties of line, the value of a curve, of balance and mass, proportion and appropriate scale.

Mr. Morris had several typical ancient types photographed upon a large scale so as to more easily compare their design and structure, and founded his own designs for his Kelmscott founts more or less upon them, giving them, whether Roman or Gothic, a distinctive character of their own. This is about as near as one can get in our conscious, selective way to old methods, in which individuals from time to time introduced small variations, while adhering to the general style and form, so that the collective traditional influence and historic continuity is preserved with the cumulative advantages of individual invention.

Of the placing of the type-page upon the paper, regarding the double page of the open book as the true unit, I have before spoken, and a great deal of art comes into the setting of the type, so as to disperse it without leaving "rivers" or gaps—much as a designer of a repeating pattern would seek to avoid running into awkward accidental lines. Constructive principle would here come in, and should be serviceable to the printer in enabling him to preserve a pleasant and harmonious ornamental effect in his page.

The designer of printers' ornaments and book illustrations, too, if he wishes to make his work an essential and harmonious part of the book is, while free in his own sphere, bound to remember the conditions under which his work will be produced and seen; and, so far from regarding these conditions as restraints, should rather regard them as sources of suggestion in the treatment of his designs, making his initial letters and decorative borders and headings natural links to unite the formal ornamental element of the type-page with the informal inclosed panel of figure design which, in its treatment of line or black and white mass, may be but an extension of the same principles found in any individual letter of the type-mass. The mechanical reason for this is, of course, that it simplifies the process of printing, type and woodcut being subject to the same pressure.

With good paper and ink, with good, well-cut type and woodcut ornaments and illustrations, the success of the book now depends upon the actual printer, as defective printing, poor impressions, the blocks not up to full strength, the impressions blurred, would spoil the effect of the best work. Bright, clean impressions are wanted, and much care and skill are required to secure such, as well as time to allow the sheets to dry well before being made up into book form.

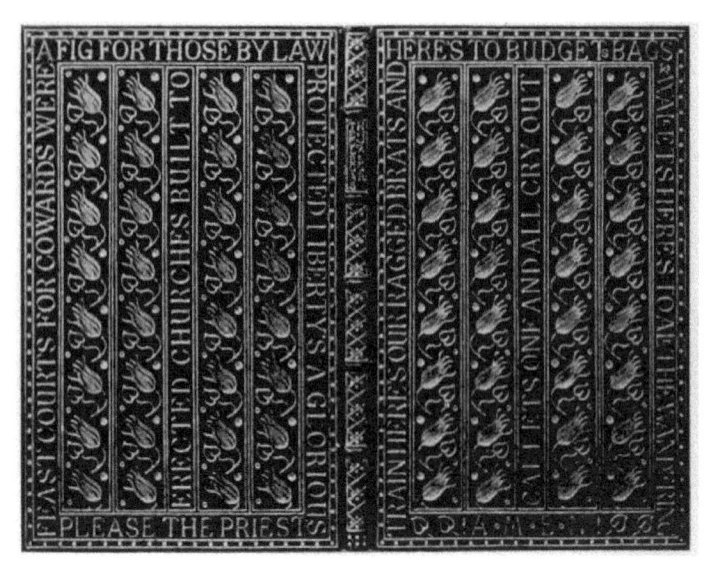

GOLD-TOOLED BOOK COVER. DESIGNED BY T. J. COBDEN-SANDERSON.

Finally the binder takes up the tale of collective skill necessary to the production of that one of the most beautiful of beautiful things—a beautiful book.

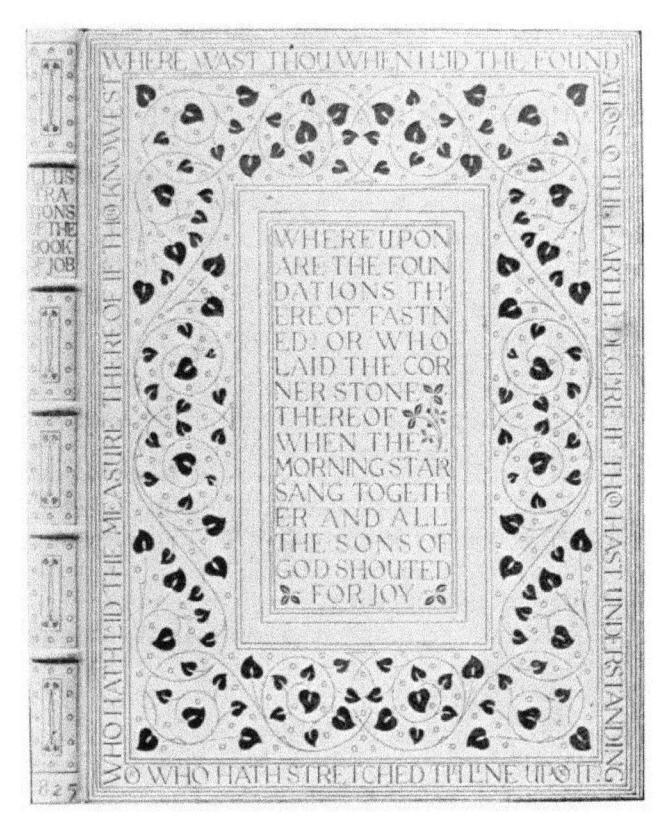

GOLD-TOOLED BOOK COVER. DESIGNED BY T. J. COBDEN-SANDERSON.

Here, of course, an immense amount of art may be called in over and above neat and careful craftsmanship in the preliminary but most necessary stages of "forwarding," as Mr. Cobden-Sanderson has told us. Beautiful binding, indeed, may display some of the most refined qualities of decorative art in disposition of line and pattern, while it affords in gold tooling another instance of strict limitation of method lending itself to free invention and fancy.

The artist is under the necessity of building up his lines and constructing his forms by the repetition of the impress of certain tools, the most resourceful designer being shown by the decorative use he is able to make of few and simple forms. An examination of the designs by Mr. Cobden-Sanderson, given here, will show that they are built up of very few units. A flower, a leaf, a stem, and straight lines of borders with the lettering, which is also an important ornamental unit. Everything depends upon the taste and skill with which they are used.

From the single example of the chain of associated labour necessary to the production of a book, we may see then how much depends upon intelligent and harmonious co-operation in collective work. Where each process is so important, where the skill and taste of each worker is so necessary to the complete result, one can hardly say that one is more important than another—certainly not less essential. We see, too, how *inter*-dependent the work of each is. Each stone in the structure must be well and truly laid, or sound progress and satisfactory completion are impossible. Art in all its manifold developments always teaches us this. Fault or failure at one stage may ruin the whole work.

Are the foundations less important than the wall; is the wall less important than the window; is the roof less essential to the house than the carving of its porch, or the painting of its interior?

If we realize the close and necessary links that unite all workers, that are essential to the production of things useful or beautiful, or both, should not we do well to strive to make the association closer and more complete than it is, and thus hand on the lamp of good tradition in design and workmanship, however far we must look forward to the enlargement of our horizon and the harmonizing of human life, and its freedom from the sinister powers and false ideals that now oppress and deceive it? And if we accept the truth that art is unity, and that what the unit is the mass may become, should we not strive, each in his sphere, whatever our main work may be, to do it worthily and well? remembering that it is better to do a small thing well than a big thing badly, and that it is the spirit in which our work is done, not the place it may accidentally occupy, or the class to which it may belong, or the reward it may receive in the ordinary estimation, that makes it great or little.

www.ingramcontent.com/pod-product-compliance
Ingram Content Group UK Ltd.
Pitfield, Milton Keynes, MK11 3LW, UK
UKHW031826270325
456796UK00002B/303